CHICAGO PUBLIC LIBRARY

Chicago Public Library
C
P
L
REFERENCE
Form 178 rev. 1-94

The Encyclopedia of
North American Indians

Volume VII

McNickle, D'Arcy – Ojibwe

General Editor
D. L. Birchfield

Marshall Cavendish
New York • London • Toronto

Published in 1997 by
Marshall Cavendish Corporation
99 White Plains Road
Tarrytown, NY 10591-9001
U.S.A.

Developed, designed, and produced by Water Buffalo Books, Milwaukee

Project director: Mark J. Sachner
General editor: D. L. Birchfield
Art director: Sabine Beaupré
Photo researcher: Diane Laska
Project editor: Valerie J. Weber

Editors: Elizabeth Kaplan, MaryLee Knowlton, Judith Plumb, Carolyn Kott Washburne

Consulting editors: Donna Beckstrom, Jack D. Forbes, Annette Reed Crum, John Bierhorst

Picture credits: © B. & C. Alexander: title, 934, 953, 1000, 1001; © Archive Photos: 882, 961, 985, 1005, 1007; © Kit Breen: 896, 932, 947, 958, 967, 968, 974, 984; © Brown Brothers, Sterling, PA: 972; © Corbis-Bettmann: 906, 907, 922, 951, 990; Photo © Addison Doty, Courtesy of Morning Star Gallery: 905; © Barry Durand, Odyssey Productions: 874 (both), 918, 982; © Eugene Fisher: Cover; © Werner Forman/Art Resource, NY: 871, 872; © Robert Frerck, Odyssey Productions: 884, 885, 886, 903, 904, 981; © Walter Frerck, Odyssey Productions: 980; © Hampton University Archives, Hampton, Virginia: 924; © Ann Hauprich: 936 (top); © 1993 Millie Knapp: 916, 956; © 1995 Millie Knapp: 925, 957; McCord Museum of Canadian History, Notman Photographic Archives: 890, 976; Milwaukee Public Museum: 928; © Kevin O. Mooney, Odyssey Productions: 979; © Sally Myers Photography 1996: 950; © Tom Myers Photography 1996: 942, 948, 949, 952, 965; New Hampshire Historical Society #389: 977; © Leslie M. Newman: 891; © Elaine Querry: 877; © Elliott Smith: 962; © STOCK MONTAGE, INC.: 902, 908, 909, 986, 993; © Stephen Trimble: 876, 878, 879, 897, 898, 926, 933, 938, 939, 945, 959, 960, 963, 964, 969, 970; University of Arkansas Museum: 900; © UPI/Corbis-Bettmann: 892, 893, 912, 913, 915, 919, 935, 940, 955, 971, 996; © 1993 S. Kay Young: 936 (bottom); © 1995 S. Kay Young: 869

Library of Congress Cataloging-in-Publication Data

The encyclopedia of North American Indians.
p. cm.
Includes bibliographical references and index.
Summary: A comprehensive reference work on the culture and history of Native Americans.
ISBN 0-7614-0234-9 (vol. 7) ISBN 0-7614-0227-6 (lib. bdg.: set)
1. Indians of North America--Encyclopedias, Juvenile.
[1. Indians of North America--Encyclopedias.]
E76.2.E53 1997
970.004'97'003--dc20 96-7700
CIP
AC

Printed and bound in Italy

Title page illustration: An Inuit hunter in Igloolik, Northwest Territories, Canada, pulls aside the brick over the door to his igloo, which serves as a temporary shelter during his hunting expedition. A historic land claim settlement between the Inuit and the Canadian government will result in the creation of a new Inuit territory, carved out of the eastern half of the Northwest Territories in Canada, to be called Nunavut. Nunavut's official birth is scheduled for April 1, 1999, giving self-determination to seventeen thousand of Canada's twenty-five thousand Inuit people. Nunavut (meaning "our land" in Inuktitut) will cover approximately one-fifth of Canada's land mass.

Editor's note: Many systems of dating have been used by different cultures throughout history. *The Encyclopedia of North American Indians* uses B.C.E. (Before Common Era) and C.E. (Common Era) instead of B.C. (Before Christ) and A.D. (Anno Domini, "In the Year of the Lord") out of respect for the diversity of the world's peoples.

Contents

McNICKLE, D'ARCY (1904–1977)

D'Arcy McNickle, a member of the Confederated Salish (or Flathead) and Kootenai Tribes, was born in St. Ignatius on the Flathead Indian Reservation in western Montana. When he was of school age, he was sent to a federal Indian boarding school in Chemewa, Oregon, where he and other children were often punished for speaking their Indian languages. This was not uncommon in the early part of the twentieth century.

After high school, at the age of seventeen, D'Arcy McNickle attended the University of Montana, where he studied anthropology and history, and then spent a year (1925–1926) at Oxford University in England.

McNickle wrote many books, including four books on American Indian culture and history, but he is best known for his novel *The Surrounded*, in which a young Indian man named Archilde, just like McNickle himself, returns to the reservation where he grew up after years of being away living in large cities. In the novel, which was published in 1936, McNickle's own life is the model for the story, which takes place on the Flathead Indian Reservation on which he was born and raised. The book is a fairly true account of life on reservations where people are poor and are not well educated.

Later, McNickle served as an administrator in the Bureau of Indian Affairs (BIA), as a professor of anthropology at the University of Saskatchewan in Canada, as the founding director of the Newberry Library Center for the History of the American Indian, and as one of the founders of the National Congress of American Indians.

SEE ALSO:
Activism, Indian; Boarding Schools; Bureau of Indian Affairs.

MEANS, RUSSELL (1940–)

Russell Means was born in Porcupine, South Dakota, on the Pine Ridge Reservation, and raised in Oakland, California, where he was trained as an accountant. His father was part Oglala and part Irish, and his mother was Yankton Sioux. In addition to his career as a public accountant, Means was a ballroom dance instructor, Native dancer, and rodeo rider before returning to South Dakota to work at the Rosebud Reservation. He moved to Cleveland, where he became director of the Cleveland Indian Center and was instrumental in turning it into the Cleveland chapter of AIM, the American Indian Movement.

Known for his charisma and his outspoken nature regarding issues of Native religious, land,

Russell Means, American Indian Movement (AIM) organizer, actor, singer, and longtime activist for Native causes, as shown in a 1995 photograph taken in Detroit.

and social rights, Means soon became one of AIM's principal spokespersons. When, in February 1972, an Oglala man, Raymond Yellow Thunder, was beaten to death in Nebraska, Means led a convoy of several hundred cars to Nebraska, where AIM members and supporters demanded the arrest of the men who had committed the murder. Means and AIM succeeded in getting the local police chief dismissed and beginning a dialogue between Natives and local residents over racial issues.

In January 1973, during an altercation in a Custer, South Dakota, courthouse between AIM and police in which an Indian man, Wesley Bad Bull Heart, was killed by a non-Native South Dakotan, the Federal Bureau of Investigation (FBI) assigned dozens of U.S. marshals to Pine Ridge to monitor Native activity and enforce security. In response to this action, Means and several hundred others traveled to Wounded Knee, the site of a massacre of hundreds of Indian people by U.S. soldiers in 1890, to protest federal intervention on Indian land and to demand recognition of Indian tribes as sovereign nations.

Surrounded by government agents, the protesters found themselves involved in a drawn-out siege that would leave two Indians dead and a marshal paralyzed. During the occupation at Wounded Knee, Means and Dennis Banks became the AIM leaders who were the most visible to the national media and AIM membership alike. In addition to playing an instrumental role in negotiating the end of the seige with government representatives, Means gained a great deal of recognition for the firmness of his convictions and beliefs, for which he stated he was prepared to die.

Between 1973 and 1980, Means was tried in at least four cases on matters related to his political activism, spent a year in prison in South Dakota, and has survived several stabbings and shootings by prisoners and others. Following a February 1974 election for Lakota tribal chairperson in which Means was barely defeated in a bitterly contested (and, some say, rigged) race by anti-AIM candidate Dick Wilson, tensions escalated when Wilson's supporters terrorized AIM members and ordered Means's supporters off the reservation. During this time of turmoil, Means was shot in the kidney by a BIA officer and, in addition to six other charges pending against him, was arraigned for assault. In recent years, AIM has been split into opposing factions, and Means has attempted to reduce his role in the movement, although he has frequently been called back to play a leadership role.

In the 1980s, Means took on a number of causes, including that of Miskito Indians persecuted by the government of Nicaragua. He also played a major role in the effort to set up Yellow Thunder Camp, a settlement of eighty structures in the Black Hills of South Dakota that has since become embroiled in legal controversy. Means also began a profitable acting career that has led to roles in several popular films. He starred as Chingkachgook, the Mohican father, in *The Last of the Mohicans*, and also appeared in *Natural Born Killers* and *Wagons East*, and his voice "appeared" in Walt Disney's *Pocahontas*.

SEE ALSO:
American Indian Movement; Banks, Dennis; Bellecourt, Clyde and Vernon; Black Hills; Bureau of Indian Affairs; Butler, Darrelle; *Incident at Oglala;* Peltier, Leonard; Wounded Knee (1890); Wounded Knee, Confrontation at (1973).

MEDICINE, INDIAN

SEE Indian Medicines; Native American Contributions.

MEDICINE SOCIETIES

In many Native American cultures, medicine societies acted as trustees of ritual activities for the good of the community. Most Native American tribes had sacred societies that cured people of diseases, chased away evil and negative beings, and turned back natural catastrophes. These organizations acted as intermediaries between spirit guides and people who were ill. Each society honored different animal spirits, invoked through very particular songs and rituals. The Zuni Coyote Society, for example, consisted of excellent hunters who cured illnesses caused by deer. When a society received an invitation to cure, it usually followed a ritual pattern of actions, beginning, for example, with a thanksgiving address and followed by the burning of tobacco as an invocation in honor of the spirits, a program of songs and dances, a blessing bestowed upon those participating, and, to end the meeting, a feast for everyone.

The Bear Society, the Buffalo Society, the Eagle Society, and the False Faces are examples of Iroquois societies. Each society had its own creation story that recounted its most important rites. False Face members, for example, made turtle-shell rattles and carved masks of wood. They burned tobacco to honor the spirits. According to certain creation accounts, these important acts became related to one another in the course of an agreement that False Face reached with the Creator. He claimed that if humans could summon him from anywhere by making carvings of his face, calling him grandfather, rattling a turtle-shell rattle like his own, making tobacco offerings, and giving him mush, then they, too, should have the ability to cure disease.

A mask used in ceremonies of the Iroquois False Face societies. This mask is carved out of wood and has braids. Smaller masks, such as the one that is attached to this one, were often used by society members as protective charms.

In addition to the ritualized actions whose purpose becomes clear in the telling of a creation story, there are also ways by which a person could become a member of a society. A dream or vision might suggest a society to an individual, who would then submit himself or herself to the rites of that society, thereby gaining membership. If a hunter dreamed of a wooden mask, for instance, heard rattling, or had legendary visions of strange faces in trees, his soul was expressing a desire to become a False Face member. Anyone needing and receiving a society's healing might eventually become a member of that society, by virtue of having gone from a weak, human state to an almost supernatural state of healing. Each society had its own symptoms that might qualify a person for healing and membership. Toothaches, nosebleeds, red spots on the face, attempting to brush imaginary hair off the face, any ailments of the head, shoulders, and joints fell

The ritual equipment of a shaman, or healer, as displayed on this carved model from the Tsimshian people of the Pacific Northwest. The equipment consists of a carved staff, a rattle, a necklace, and a bear-claw crown.

under the jurisdiction of the False Faces. When a patient complained to the elders of the tribe, they prescribed a society accordingly.

The Pueblo Indians had medicine societies that healed sicknesses resulting from spiritual causes or witchcraft. Some societies used sacred objects, such as jimsonweed, tobacco, nettles, and red ants. Women were allowed to be members of these societies, but they were not allowed to cure. To become a member, a person either volunteered or was trapped, or ritually captured, after entering a sacred area as defined by a society while it was performing. Often, as in the case of the Iroquois, a sick person was taken into the society after a vow made during illness or recovery. Each Pueblo society had a special chamber where initiations and retreats were held. Many groups performed at important community events like the Kachina rain dances. Clowns were influential priests who showed up at this and other ceremonies, adding a comic element.

In some tribes, particular healers or medicine persons were ranked into societies. The Ojibwes (Chippewas) had their highest-ranking priests in the Midewiwin society. The next society in line was the Wabenos, or dawn men, who, among other things, practiced medical magic and hunting medicine and created love powders. Next in line following the Wabenos was the Jessakid society, which included prophets and seers, followed by herbalists or Mashkikike-winini, in a fourth group.

Entering a society was thought to protect a member who had once been close to death because of illness, accidents, or the violation of a taboo. This member could then help cure others.

Not all medicine persons belonged to medical societies; many performed independently as individuals. And the societies did have other responsibilities, such as controlling the weather or conducting certain ceremonies. Whatever their responsibilities, they remained under the strict control of a chief and several officers, structuring and binding a community in powerful ways.

MEECH LAKE ACCORD

Canadian Natives threw a political monkey wrench into the workings of the Meech Lake Accord in 1990. The accord would have given Quebec—which is culturally, linguistically, and ethnically mostly French in character—a "special status" designation in the Canadian confederation. The accord was thus meant to satisfy Quebec's demands for autonomy within primarily English-speaking Canada. While granting Quebec special status, however, the accord would have avoided acknowledging another important "special" Canadian group—Native peoples—and their original occupancy of Quebec and the rest of Canada.

Elijah Harper, the only Native member of Manitoba's legislature, led an effort against ratification of the Meech Lake Accord by its deadline of June 23, 1990. His vote, which was motivated by Native Canadians' anger over their omission from the accord, started a chain of legal procedures that ultimately prevented the accord from going into effect.

Konrad Sioui, head chief of the Assembly of First Nations, has said that the rising tide of Native anger across Canada was evidence of a belief that Quebec should not become a nation until it recognizes that it is built on land stolen from the first nations (Native peoples), that its economy is based on resources also taken from Native people, and that the entire Canadian governmental system for negotiating land claims ought to be revamped. Native Canadians were also demanding that Quebec and other provinces be prepared to rectify past injustices.

Eighty-five percent of Quebec never has been signed away from Native peoples by treaty. Although leaders of the Quebec independence movement at least pay lip service to the idea that any constitution for an independent Quebec should respect Native land claims as an issue of minority-group justice, there are still many issues left to divide Native and French Canadians. It is unlikely, for example, that many French Canadians are willing to take seriously the Natives' assertion that French Canadians' claim to the province should not extend much beyond the Montreal and Quebec City urban areas.

SEE ALSO:
Kahnawake Mohawks; Quebec.

MENOMINEE

According to Menominee oral history, the Menominee people originated from a Great Bear and other animals in spiritual form that emerged from beneath the earth on the western shores of Green Bay, in the present-day state of Wisconsin. The Menominees (sometimes spelled "Menomini") have lived in the area ever since.

Before they had contact with Euro-Americans, the Menominees lived in settled villages. Their staple foods were wild rice and fish. In 1634, Samuel de Champlain, governor of New France, sent Sieur Jean Nicolet to negotiate peace with the Winnebagos, who also lived near Green Bay. Nicolet became the first European to encounter the Menominees. Within a few decades, the area was visited by French trappers, who paid the Indians to capture fur-bearing animals for them. The Menominees scattered into small mobile bands for the fur trade. Until about 1760, the area the Menominees lived in was under mainly French influence.

In 1761, the British replaced the French in Menominee Country during the French and Indian War. The area was ceded to the United States by Britain in 1794 as part of the Jay Treaty, but the first U.S. citizens did not arrive in the area until about 1815.

One of the best-known Menominee chiefs at this time was Oshkosh (1795–1858), namesake of a city between Milwaukee and Green Bay in present-day Wisconsin. Son of a Menominee chief, Oshkosh was born at Old King's Village on the Fox River. He first went to war at age seventeen in support of British troops in the War of 1812, taking part in the attack on Fort Mackinaw, Wisconsin, and Fort Stephenson, Ohio. Oshkosh switched allegiance to the U.S. side in Black Hawk's War with the Sac and Fox Nations, after which he was recognized by the United States as treaty chief for the Menominees.

Oshkosh's support of the American cause did not keep the federal government from forcing his hand diplomatically in 1848, when he signed the Treaty of Lake Powahekone, ceding much of the Menominees' land base in Wisconsin. Oshkosh became alcoholic with age; he also came to weigh almost 400 pounds (180 kilograms). Oshkosh was once said to have murdered a man without provocation while drunk, and he died in a drunken brawl with another Indian man at Keshena, Wisconsin, in 1858. In 1911, a statue depicting a slim and sober Oshkosh at the prime of his life (about thirty-five years old) was erected in Oshkosh, Wisconsin.

Between 1830 and 1850, the non-Indian population of Wisconsin rose from about four thousand to three hundred thousand. Much of the Menominees' land was ceded in a series of treaties; they were left with a 270,000-acre (109,350-hectare) reservation. This continued to be their home for a century, until the Menominees became targets of "termination," the result of a congressional act that broke up their land base.

The Menominees shared ownership of property valued at $34 million when their termination

bill was enacted in 1953. By 1961, the federal government was out of Menominee Country, and each member of the former tribe had become the owner of one hundred shares of stock and a negotiable bond valued at $3,000, issued in the name of Menominee Enterprises, Inc. (MEI). This entity held the former tribe's land and businesses. Governmentally, the Menominee Nation had become Menominee County, the smallest (in terms of population) and poorest (in terms of cash income) in Wisconsin.

As a county, Menominee had to raise taxes to pay for its share of services, including welfare, health services, utilities, and so on. The only taxable business in the county was MEI, which was forced to raise the funds to pay its tax bill by restructuring so that stockholders had to buy their homes and the property on which they had been built. Most of the Menominees had little savings except for their $3,000 bonds, which were then sold to MEI to make the required home purchases. Many Menominees thus faced private-sector health costs, property taxes, and other expenses with no more money than they had had before termination. Unemployment rose to levels that most of the United States had known only during the Depression of the 1930s.

By 1965, health indicators in Menominee County sounded like a reprint of the Meriam Report, which almost four decades earlier had documented how badly Native people under the government's care had been treated. Tuberculosis afflicted nearly 35 percent of the population, and infant mortality was three times the national average. Termination, like allotment, had been an abject failure at anything other than taking Indian land.

Left: Two photographic portraits taken at a Menominee gathering in Wisconsin. The man in the bottom photo has incorporated the American flag into his regalia in several ways.

The Menominees fought termination. In 1968, in *Menominee Tribe v. United States*, the U.S. Supreme Court held that Menominee hunting and fishing rights survived the termination of the tribe by Congress. Thus, Wisconsin was not allowed to enforce its fishing and game laws against individual Menominees.

In 1973, President Richard M. Nixon signed the Menominee Restoration Act, which allowed reservation status again on the Menominees' 233,900-acre (95,560-hectare) land base in northern Wisconsin about forty miles (sixty-four kilometers) west of Green Bay. By the late 1980s, the Menominees had established extensive gaming operations that funded new tribal health and welfare measures and drew many people back to the reservation. By 1992, 7,100 people were enrolled as Menominees, twice the number before termination. About half lived on the reservation.

— B. E. Johansen

SEE ALSO:
Black Hawk; Meriam, Lewis; Termination Policy; Winnebago; Wisconsin.

MERIAM, LEWIS (1883–1972)

Dr. Lewis Meriam, an employee of the Brookings Institution, was the primary author of a comprehensive report on reservation social and economic conditions compiled in the middle 1920s and released in 1928. Meriam himself went on to write several different reports on different aspects of United States governmental administration. The Meriam Report, funded by a grant from the John D. Rockefeller Foundation, helped stimulate efforts to elevate Indians' health and welfare in the 1930s. The Meriam Report documented the horrid condition of human health and welfare under the Bureau of Indian Affairs' "wardship."

By 1923, an organized committee of influential Indians and non-Indians, called "the Committee of One Hundred," was lobbying for more respectful and humane treatment of surviving American Indians. Among its members were John Collier, William Jennings Bryan, Clark Wissler, General John J. Pershing, Bernard Baruch, William Allen White, and Arthur C. Parker. Parker, who was an Iroquois, was elected presiding officer of the group at a convention in Washington, D.C., during December of 1923. Under his direction, in 1924, the group published its findings under the title *The Indian Problem*. This document formed the basis for the better-known Meriam Report four years later.

The report provided graphic evidence of just how badly their government's "wards" were being treated. Infant mortality on Indian reservations, for example, was found to be nearly three times that of European-descended Americans. Large numbers of Indians were dying from tuberculosis, measles, and other diseases that had been largely eradicated in mainstream society. In this sea of disease, health services on reservations were ill-equipped and lacking in sufficiently trained staff. Diets heavy on cheap-commodity carbohydrates (the kind found in high-calorie junk food) were producing malnutrition in people who were otherwise overweight. The government provided 11 cents a day to feed students at its boarding schools and skimped on equipment and salaries for teachers. Schools were often unsanitary. Per-capita income for Native reservation residents was less than $200 a year at a time when national average earnings were $1,350 a year.

The belief that government should address its mistakes with regard to Indian affairs became a popular political theme after the release of the Meriam Report. Even before John Collier became Indian commissioner, a liberal tendency was evident under the otherwise conservative presidency of Herbert Hoover. Hoover drew the distinguished and articulate Ray Lyman from the presidency of Stanford University to become his secretary of the interior. Hoover also chose Charles J. Rhoades, a devout Quaker, as commissioner of Indian Affairs. Rhoades quickly set about trying to implement the findings of the Meriam Report. Thus began some momentum for radical reforms inside the Bureau of Indian Affairs, which Collier's tenure hastened.

SEE ALSO:
Bureau of Indian Affairs; Collier, John; Infant Death Rate; Parker, Arthur; Social Conditions, Contemporary.

MERIAM REPORT

SEE Meriam, Lewis.

MESA VERDE

Mesa Verde is a national park in southwestern Colorado. It contains the most spectacular Anasazi cliff dwellings, including Cliff Palace, the largest cliff dwelling in the Southwest, with more than two hundred rooms and twenty-three kivas, or underground ceremonial chambers.

A rugged country of deep canyons and high mesa tops, the Mesa Verde plateau is at the northern edge of the Anasazi country. The Anasazis were relatively late in occupying the plateau. The earliest recorded Mesa Verde site dates to 608 C.E. Other Anasazi sites only fifty miles (eighty kilometers) away are as much as eight hundred years older.

For most of their tenure on the Mesa Verde plateau, the Anasazis lived only on the tops of the mesas. It was not until the thirteenth century that some of the Anasazis moved down into the canyons and built the cliff dwellings. Even then, many Anasazis remained on top of the mesas.

The tops of the mesas have a longer growing season than the depths of the valleys below, long enough for growing corn. In normal times, the mesas receive enough rainfall for agriculture, about eighteen inches (forty-six centimeters) annually. They were originally well-timbered with Douglas fir and were abundant with deer, bighorn sheep, and cottontail rabbits.

The great mystery of Mesa Verde has always been why it was abandoned by the Anasazis in the last decades of the thirteenth century. Successive generations of archaeological inquiry have now taken most of the mystery out of the exodus. It now appears that the Anasazis simply depleted the resources of their environment to a point where they could not sustain their population during a prolonged drought, such as the one that occurred in the late thirteenth century.

The Spruce Tree House ruins at Mesa Verde, Colorado, as seen in winter.

The interplay of natural rock formations, evergreen vegetation, rugged terrain, and the ruins of ancient Anasazi dwellings make Mesa Verde a fascinating and complex remnant of an early American culture.

The evidence of environmental depletion is most easily seen by comparing early Mesa Verde sites with later ones. At the early sites, Douglas fir accounts for 30 percent of the timber used for roof beams; at the later sites, the percentage drops to 3 percent. As the forests were depleted and hunting pressure increased, the wildlife changed. Early sites show a consumption of bison, bighorn sheep, and mule deer; later sites show a dependence on rabbit, squirrel, and domestic turkey for meat. Where rabbits are concerned, early sites contain bones of the cottontail rabbit, a species that inhabits brush and woodland country; later sites contain bones of the jackrabbit, a species that inhabits open brush country.

In addition to Cliff Palace, other noteworthy structures at Mesa Verde National Park include Cedar Tree Tower, Square Tower House, Balcony House, and Spruce Tree House, some of which are better preserved than Cliff Palace. The park also has a museum and a lodge.

SEE ALSO:
Anasazi; Cliff Dwellings; Colorado; Kiva.

MESCALERO APACHE

The Mescalero Apache Reservation consists of 460,000 acres (184,000 hectares) in southeastern New Mexico, in the Sacramento Mountains northeast of Alamogordo. Tribal headquarters are in Mescalero, New Mexico. The reservation is located in the heart of a mountain recreational area, with much of the adjacent land consisting of the Lincoln National Forest.

The Mescaleros have taken advantage of the scenic beauty to bring tourist dollars into their economy with such tribal enterprises as a ski area and a large resort. The nearby Ruidoso Downs horseracing track also brings visitors to the area. From mid-May to mid-September, lake and stream fishing is available at Eagle Creek Lakes, Silver Springs, and Rio Ruidoso recreation areas.

The Mescaleros, like the Jicarillas, are an Eastern Apache tribe, with many cultural influences from the Southern Great Plains. The Mescalero name derives from their most famous food, baked mescal, a large desert agave plant, which is a traditional Apache food. It is still occasionally harvested

Fishing on the Mescalero Apache Reservation in Mescalero, New Mexico.

Sierra Blanca rises majestically over the Mescalero Apache Reservation in New Mexico. In the foreground is the Inn of the Mountain Gods, one of several resorts that attract visitors and provide employment to the Mescaleros.

and prepared. The proper harvesting season is in May or June when massive red flowers begin to appear in the mescal patches, which cannot be located without specialized knowledge. The plant is dug out of the ground and stripped, leaving a white bulb two to three feet (sixty-one to ninety-one centimeters) in circumference. A large cooking pit is dug, about fifteen feet (almost three meters) long, four feet (over one meter) wide and four feet (over one meter) deep, large enough to cook about two thousand pounds (nine hundred kilograms) of mescal. The bottom of the pit is lined with stones, on top of which fires are built. The mescal is placed on top of the stones, then covered with a layer of straw and then a layer of dirt. When cooked, the mescal is a fibrous, sticky, syrupy substance with a flavor similar to molasses. Portions are also dried in thin layers, which can last indefinitely without spoiling, providing the Apaches with lightweight rations for extended journeys.

Many members of the Mescalero Apaches find employment at their ski resort, Ski Apache. Others work at the tribal museum and visitor center in Mescalero, New Mexico. A large Mescalero enterprise, the Inn of the Mountain Gods has a gift shop, horseback riding, skeet and trap shooting, tennis, several restaurants, and an eighteen-hole golf course. The Mescalero Apaches maintain three campgrounds near Ruidoso, New Mexico—Cienegita Lakes, Eagle Creek Lakes, and Ruidoso Creek. Another campground, Silver Springs, is near Cloudcroft, New Mexico. The Mescalero Apache Gahan Ceremonial occurs each year on July 1 through 4 at Mescalero, New Mexico.

SEE ALSO:
Apache; Jicarilla Apache; New Mexico.

MESQUAKIE (FOX)

The Mesquakies are an Algonquian nation, commonly called "Fox" by Europeans, who were closely allied with the Sauk (also known as Sac) during the expansion of European colonization. By the late twentieth century, a small group of Mesquakies lived near Tama, Iowa; others lived with the Sauks in Oklahoma. In their own language, Mesquakie means "people of the red earth."

About 1820, the Fox and Sauk divided over whether to resist Euro-American expansion into their country in what is now southern Illinois. Keokuk and a number of his supporters decided to accommodate the expansion, as they moved into Iowa. The Sauk Black Hawk (Makataimeshekiakiak; c. 1770–1838) and his supporters remained at their principal village, Saukenuk, at the confluence of the Rock and Mississippi Rivers, the site of present-day Rock Island. The land provided abundant crops and the river was a rich source of fish. Black Hawk consulted with the spiritual leaders White Cloud and Neapope, who advised him to seek allies in defense of the land.

Keokuk (c. 1783–1848) was recognized by United States officials after he refused to support Black Hawk during the years before and after Black Hawk's War (1832). Born in the village of Saukenuk, Keokuk's mother was half French, so he could not be an hereditary chief. He obtained his position through merit, notably by his bravery against the Sioux, as well as by working out political arrangements with invading whites.

In the meantime, George Davenport, the Indian agent in the area, had purchased the site on which Saukenuk was built, including Black Hawk's own lodge and his people's graveyard. U.S. colonizers began to take land around the village. Illinois Governor John Reynolds ordered the state militia to march on Saukenuk. Black Hawk and his band moved west across the Mississippi, but they pledged to return.

Regular U.S. Army troops were brought in to pursue Black Hawk's band, whose members had been forced to subsist on roots in the swamplands near the Mississippi. Several army and militia units caught Black Hawk and his people, their backs to the river, having hoisted a flag of truce. General Winfield Scott and other officers ignored the appeal for a truce, and engaged in a one-sided slaughter that became known as the Battle of Black Ax. General Scott later apologized for the large number of women and children killed by his men. He claimed that they could not be distinguished from warriors in the heat of battle.

Black Hawk, Neapope, and other survivors of the battle fled north to a Winnebago village, where they were betrayed for a bribe of twenty horses and one hundred dollars.

After Black Hawk's War, President Andrew Jackson recognized Keokuk, instead of Black Hawk, as chief of the Sac and Fox. Initially outraged by this decision, Black Hawk eventually settled on land governed by Keokuk, near Iowaville on the Des Moines River. Shortly before his death, in 1838, Black Hawk acknowledged his defeat without lingering bitterness, telling a Fourth of July gathering near Fort Madison that he wished past conflicts to be "buried" and "forgotten" and acknowledging that Rock River, "the home of my people," now belonged to his former enemies. "Keep it as we did," he urged his listeners; "it will produce you good crops."

SEE ALSO:
Black Hawk; Jackson, Andrew; Keokuk; Sac and Fox.

MÉTIS

The Métis people are of mixed European and Indian blood; their culture arose as a result of the fur-trading industry in early Canada. Although the Métis represent many different backgrounds, the cultural group that emerged was typically descended from French fathers and Cree or Ojibwe (Chippewa) mothers. They originally settled near the Great Lakes, with a large center of population in the Red River area, where present-day Winnipeg, Manitoba, now lies.

The Métis occupied an important place in early Canadian history and commerce. They were fur trappers and provided supplies for the two large trading companies, the Hudson's Bay Company and the North West Company. The Métis participated in an annual communal buffalo hunt, which became an important part of their society. After the dramatic kills, the buffalo meat was dried and made into pemmican (a Native food made from lean, dried strips of meat pounded into a paste, mixed with animal fat and berries, and pressed into small cakes). The pemmican, in turn, was sold to the trading companies.

In 1812, the Hudson's Bay Company, which owned most of modern Manitoba, granted colonists land along the Red River for an agricultural settlement. The Métis organized under Cuthbert Grant to oppose the new colonists, who had outlawed buffalo hunting and pemmican sales. They clashed at the Battle of Seven Oaks, which left the colony's governor and twenty settlers dead, as well as one Métis man. The Métis continued their lifestyle.

The two rival fur-trading companies combined in 1821 under the Hudson's Bay Company, which sought to sell the Red River area to Canada in 1869. Fearing they would lose much in this transaction, the Métis under Louis Riel seized Fort Garry. They declared a provisional government to negotiate the terms under which they would join Canada, including a demand for title to 1.4 million acres (560,000 hectares) of land. The Manitoba Act of 1870 was based on these negotiations, but because of resulting fraud and blunder, few Métis ended up with land in Manitoba. In addition, the buffalo and fur-bearing animals were gone. Many Métis left the area to head farther west, where they could maintain their traditional lifestyle.

A number of Métis communities arose near the fork of the Saskatchewan River, but again, they feared the loss of their land, animals, and possessions by incoming settlers. Gabriel Dumont called Louis Riel to Saskatchewan to help them in 1885, and the Métis followed the same pattern at Red River by seizing a parish church and again establishing a provisional government. This Northwest Rebellion lasted two months, during which the Métis were joined by other Native people defending their lands. Shaken at the thought of a general Indian uprising, the Canadian government sent large numbers of troops to the area. At the Battle of Batoche, a few hundred Métis held off a thousand better-armed soldiers for four days, but the government forces prevailed.

The Métis scattered again, some going even deeper into the wilderness to continue their traditional life of hunting and trapping. Others merged with Indian groups and lived with the treaty Indians. Still others lived on the fringes of the settlements on unallotted land belonging to England and became known as "road allowance people."

The Métis were not eligible for Native reserves and programs, and yet they were shut out of mainstream Canadian life. They lived in relative poverty, occupied with odd jobs when hunting and trapping no longer made a living. Even so, their culture was unique. The men were known for their skill as fiddlers and dancers, the women for their elaborate flowered beadwork.

In the 1930s, the Métis Association was formed to bring the conditions of the Métis to the government's attention. As a result, the Métis Betterment Act passed in 1938. Twelve Métis colonies were established in Alberta. These colonies, eight of which still exist, are similar to the Native reserves. This was the only communally owned land base the Métis had for a long time. The Canadian government settled a Métis suit in 1989 that gave the Métis full title to the Alberta lands and a cash settlement.

Most provinces now have Métis Associations, and the Canadian government now includes the Métis in land claims settlements. In 1986, the Manitoba Métis began a legal action against the government in order to recover the lands that had been allocated to the Métis by the Manitoba Act of 1870 but subsequently denied them. A 1990 Supreme Court of Canada ruling allowed them to proceed with the suit, which involves a great deal of land in downtown Winnipeg.

The term *Métis* is now being more widely applied and includes anyone with partial Indian heritage, as well as all nonstatus Indians (that is, Native people who do not belong to a tribe recogninzed by the Canadian government). Political activity has raised the consciousness of many Canadians about the Métis, who continue to act as a vital force in the country.

— M. A. Stout

SEE ALSO:

Alberta; British Columbia Association of Non-Status Indians; Buffalo; Canada, Native–Non-Native Relations in; France; Hudson's Bay Company; Manitoba; North West Company; Ojibwe; Riel, Louis; Saskatchewan.

MEXICAN-AMERICAN WAR

The United States and Mexico had a number of grievances against one another in the 1840s. U.S.

The Battle of Molino del Rey in the Mexican-American War. The United States' acquisition of huge portions of Mexican territory in what is now the American Southwest had a huge impact on the lives and identities of Native people in the region.

citizens wanted compensation for property that had been seized during revolutions in Mexico. Mexicans were concerned about U.S. ambitions in what is now known as the American Southwest, ambitions that Americans could satisfy only by acquiring Mexican national territory west of the newly founded Republic of Texas. The United States openly coveted California and attempted to purchase that Mexican province, but Mexico declined to negotiate such a sale. Mexicans and Texans also disagreed about the boundary separating their countries. The Texans claimed the Rio Grande as their southern boundary, and the Mexicans claimed that the boundary was farther north, at the Nueces River. When the United States annexed Texas in December 1845, it adopted the Texas claim that the southern boundary was the Rio Grande. When the United States moved troops into the disputed area between the Nueces River and the Rio Grande the Mexicans viewed it as an invasion of their national territory; the armed forces of the two nations clashed.

On May 13, 1846, the United States declared war on Mexico. Several U.S. armies invaded Mexican territory. General Zachary Taylor led one army from Texas across the Rio Grande into northeastern Mexico. General Stephen W. Kearny led an army west across the Great Plains from Fort Leavenworth in Kansas into the Mexican province of New Mexico and then on to California. General John E. Wood led an army from San Antonio, Texas, into northern Mexico at El Paso. General Winfield Scott landed another army at Vera Cruz on the Mexican coast of the Gulf of Mexico and fought his way inland to the national capital, Mexico City. On September 14, 1847, General Scott's army entered Mexico City, which effectively ended the war.

By the Treaty of Guadalupe Hidalgo, signed February 2, 1848, which formally ended the war,

Mexico ceded to the United States two-fifths of its territory. The boundary between Mexico and the United States became the Rio Grande from its mouth on the Gulf of Mexico to the border of New Mexico, then west to the Gila River, then down the Gila River to its confluence with the Colorado River, and then west along the boundary between the Mexican provinces of Alta (upper) and Baja (lower) California. Thus, the United States acquired its present southwestern states, including the state of California. (The southern boundaries of New Mexico and Arizona were later adjusted by an additional purchase of land known as the Gadsden Purchase.)

The acquisition of this large tract of land by the United States had a devastating effect on the indigenous peoples of the region. The Navajos in northeastern Arizona and northwestern New Mexico, who had not been seriously disturbed in their homeland by Spain or Mexico, soon found themselves confronted by the United States Army, which constructed forts, such as Fort Defiance, in the very heart of their country. By 1864, the United States Army had burned their homes and crops and had chopped down their orchards to starve them into submission to U.S. authority. More than seven thousand starving Navajos were marched hundreds of miles to a concentration camp in eastern New Mexico near Fort Sumner called Bosque Redondo, where they remained until 1868 before being allowed to return to their homeland. Their land, however, had been greatly reduced in size by the treaty of June 1, 1868. No one knows how many people died during this ordeal.

In California, the discovery of gold and the resulting gold rush brought to the region a large lawless population that had no regard for the rights of indigenous people. Tribes were pushed off their land, relocated, and sometimes simply massacred. In some portions of the state, bounties were paid for Indian scalps, and they were hunted and killed like animals.

In New Mexico, the Pueblo Indians of the upper Rio Grande Valley lost their legal status as Indians. The Treaty of Guadalupe Hidalgo stated that all citizens of Mexico who remained in the ceded land after a specified period of time automatically became citizens of the United States. Mexico had conferred citizenship on the Pueblos, and thus the United States claimed that the Pueblos were now U.S. citizens. This legal maneuver was used by the people of New Mexico to divest the Pueblos of much of their land and water rights, until the Pueblos finally gained a Supreme Court ruling that reestablished their legal status as Indians.

Throughout the area encompassed by the Treaty of Guadalupe Hidalgo, indigenous peoples soon found themselves in confrontation with non-Indians surging west, expanding the American frontier. The indigenous populations soon found their cultures, languages, religions, land bases, and their means of livelihood under assault by a people determined to impose their culture upon them.

— D. L. Birchfield

SEE ALSO:

Arizona; Bosque Redondo; California; Gold Rush; Guadalupe Hidalgo, Treaty of; Long Walk; Navajo; Mexico, Indigenous Peoples of; New Mexico; New Spain; Pueblo; Texas.

MEXICAN-AMERICANS

SEE Latinos.

MEXICO, INDIGENOUS PEOPLES OF

In the Valley of Mexico, complex civilizations began to organize at about the time that the Roman Empire was expanding across Europe, Northern Africa, and Palestine, at the beginning of the Common Era (the time following the birth of Christ). These civilizations would rise and fall over the centuries at different locations in the valley that now contains Mexico City. A series of empire-building city-states had been rising and falling for more than fifteen hundred years when, in 1519, Hernán Cortés met the Aztecs, whose empire was perhaps the most far-reaching of them all. Today, Mexico is a combination of Spanish and Indian heritages, including, in addition to the Aztec, the Maya, Zapotec, Mixtec, Yaqui, Tarahumara, Huichol, and others.

Archaeological evidence indicates highly developed societies with military and religious elites sup-

In this wall mural by Mexican artist Diego Rivera in Oaxaca (pronounced *wah-HAH-cah),* in southern Mexico, ancient Mixtec scholars study religious and cultural stories depicted in elaborately illustrated works of art called codices. Codices, which were bound in book form, were painted on animal hides.

ported by intensive agriculture in an area that was probably much more lush than Mexico City appears today. During the last five hundred years, vegetation has been stunted by the overgrazing of sheep imported from Europe. In the twentieth century, air pollution also has stunted the growth of vegetation in the Valley of Mexico.

More than a century before the birth of Christ, the first true urban areas in North America arose in the Valley of Mexico, at Teotihuacán, northeast of the vast lake in which the Aztecs would later build Tenochtitlán. Another urban area arose at Cuicuilco, in the southwestern part of the Valley of Mexico, near the National University's present-day campus, on the southern side of Mexico City.

With an estimated population of about two hundred thousand, Teotihuacán (meaning "Place of the Gods" in Nahuatl, the Aztec language) was one of the largest—if not *the* largest—urban area on earth at that time, equal or nearly equal in population to the Aztec capital of Tenochtitlán more than eight hundred years later. Cities such as London and Paris did not reach that size until after Europe's Age of Exploration began more than one thousand years later. The city covered eight square miles (twenty square kilometers), with ceremonial buildings and more then two thousand large apartment blocks. Some of the apartment blocks functioned as workplaces as well as homes.

The city of Teotihuacán reached the height of its power by about 500 C.E. and declined by roughly 800 C.E., after which other cities competed for power. At about 800 C.E., or just a century before the widespread decline of Maya culture to the south, Teotihuacán seems to have been destroyed deliberately by enemies from the outside who set fires in the city.

The Aztecs believed that the world had been created and destroyed four times and that their own world, the fifth, would likewise come to an end. These cycles of life and death recalled the rise and fall of the civilizations that preceded them. One of the prior epochs was said to have occurred in Teotihuacán, whose influence passed to the Aztecs through Tula, the capital of the Toltecs, which reached its height shortly after 1000 C.E.

While the Aztecs did not originate in the Valley of Mexico, they were, in effect, absorbed by the fifteen-hundred-year-old urban tradition of the area after they arrived and conquered the descendants of Teotihuacán and other cities. The Aztecs' Great Temple contained an area (two so-called red temples) that affected Teotihuacán-style symbols, including architecture.

When the Aztecs arrived in the Valley of Mexico, several centuries after Teotihuacán had thrived there, they found a vast lake in the mountains of central Mexico. On an island in the lake, they built the grandest of Native American cities. As the Aztecs' empire spread, Tenochtitlán grew on land reclaimed from swamps. Two three-mile-long (five-kilometer-long) aqueducts were built to carry fresh water from the mainland, so one could be closed for cleaning without depriving the city of water. Tribute and captives flowed into the city after conquests that spread from the Gulf of Mexico to the Pacific.

West of the Valley of Mexico, however, the Aztecs' armies were stopped by the bowmen of the Tarascans. They also never completely conquered the Tlaxcalans to the east, although they did surround their city and cut off commerce. The Aztecs' dominance was only rarely administrative; after they pillaged another people's city, it was most often left alone to manage its own affairs—until the next call for tribute and captives.

Like few other peoples in the Americas, the Aztecs were mobilized for war, for expansion, and for the gathering of tribute from less militaristic peoples. Every Aztec man over the age of fifteen was considered to be a potential member of the army, except those in training for the priesthood or as civil officials. In practice, not all were mobilized at once.

All young boys were taught the use of basic weapons, such as the spear thrower and bow and arrow. At age fifteen, most eligible young men in Tenochtitlán were sent to live for a number of months in "houses of youth," where they were taught arts of war, as well as academic subjects. The capital city had twenty "houses of youth," each affiliated with a different administrative district, called a *calpulli*, which is a type of clan.

A family takes a break from their work at a market in southern Mexico.

This young Zapotec Indian prepares produce for sale at a popular Sunday market in Tlacolula, a town in southern Mexico.

The Aztecs governed themselves according to a clan-based system that included aspects of consensus and hierarchy. This system did not fit any European conception of government. The Aztec Nation comprised twenty clans, or *calpulli*, each of which elected officials similar to county clerks or aldermen. Each clan also elected a speaker (*tlatoani*), who sat on a supreme state council. From these leaders, four were appointed to executive posts. In Tenochtitlán, one of these four, called *tlacatecuhtli* (chief of men) or *hueytlatoani* (revered speaker) was chosen to be chief executive, a lifetime appointment. The dual nature of the system accounts for the fact that some Spanish records refer to the government as a "republic," while others designate leaders as "kings." Elected along kin lines, Aztec leaders enjoyed total authority once they were elevated to supreme office.

Ownership of most land rested with the clans. Clan ownership of land often confused the Spanish, who were accustomed to individual or royal ownership. Another concept that sometimes confused the Spanish, who came from a male-dominated society, was the influence of the Aztec women. According to William H. Prescott, in *Conquest of Mexico*, Aztec women took part in social festivities as equal partners with men. The Aztecs' many gods included both sexes in important roles. Aztec women also played a strong role in the home and in the marketplace, but they did not take an active role in politics, as did Iroquois women. They did, however, hold high offices in the Aztec religious order, and women who died in childbirth had the same status as warriors who died in battle. Women participated in the workforce as textile workers, salespersons, artists, artisans, midwives, and seamstresses. An Aztec woman of the upper class could own property in her own name.

Symbols played a very important role in the Aztec mind. Their capital was believed to be the center of the universe, and the Great Temple of Tenochtitlán was the center of Aztec spiritual and secular power. Tenochtitlán's two main temples were dedicated to the two gods who influenced the most important events and values in Mexican life: the gods of agriculture, rain, and water (Tlaloc) and of war, tribute, and conquest (Huitzilopochtli). The temples dedicated to these two gods displayed an Aztec attitude of dominance over the peoples around them—an attitude that the Spanish also displayed as they built their own religious center, a major cathedral, on top of the Great Temple.

The Aztecs' capital was full of color; the architecture was painted turquoise, yellow, red, and green and often was annotated with visual history in the form of murals. One could see the eagle, snake, and cactus that constitute Mexico's modern national symbol on some of the buildings. The Aztec maintained that they had been led to this spot by divine prophecy, to a place where an eagle perched on a cactus extended its wings toward the rays of the sun.

The fact that such a city was built in less than two centuries is wonder enough even in modern times. When one reflects on the Aztecs' lack of construction machinery (even the wheel), the scope of the metropolis that grew up here becomes even more astounding. The island on which Tenochtitlán was built contained no construction materials, so virtually everything used to construct it had to be imported to build a city that the first Spanish observers called one of the largest and most prosperous they had ever seen.

Although the Spanish conquered Mexico in a military sense, the Spanish population very quickly mixed with surviving Aztecs and other Indians. Today, most people in Mexico have some degree of indigenous blood. Mexico does not have a system of Indian reservations like the United States or reserves like Canada, but distinct Native communities still exist in many rural areas, particularly in the southern Mexican state of Chiapas, where the eviction of Native descendants of the Mayas from their homelands by agribusiness has created social and political unrest.

— B. E. Johansen

SEE ALSO:

Aztec; Latinos; Maya; Mixtec; Spain; Zapotec.

SUGGESTED READINGS:

Gyles, Anna Benson. *Of Gods and Men: Mexico and the Mexican Indians*. London: British Broadcasting Corp., 1980.

Leon-Portilla, Miguel. *The Aztec Image of Self and Society: An Introduction to Náhua Culture*. Salt Lake City: University of Utah Press, 1992.

Leon-Portilla, Miguel. *Pre-Columbian Literatures of Mexico*. Norman: University of Oklahoma Press, 1969.
Tannenbaum, Frank. *Peace by Revolution: Mexico After 1810*. [1933] New York: Columbia University Press, 1966.

MIAMI

Early European settlers and explorers referred to the Miami Indians by various names. English writers, for example, called them the "Twightwee," a name that came from the Miami word *Twa-h-twa-h*. Twa-h-Twa-h, which means "the cry of the crane," is the name the nation used for its own people. The name *Miami* actually comes from *Oumameg*, an Ojibwe (Chippewa) word meaning "people who live on the peninsula."

The Miamis initially lived in the Great Lakes region—the French met them in the 1600s in the area around present-day Green Bay, Wisconsin—but by the early 1700s, they had already begun migrating to an area south of Lake Michigan in present-day southern Indiana and southwestern Ohio. Like other Indian nations in the eighteenth century, the Miamis found themselves caught up in the prolonged conflict between France and England, which the English called the French and Indian War. The allegiances of various Native groups often shifted from one European colonial power to the other, and often members of the same nation were on opposite sides of the conflict. Along with such Great Lakes nations as the Sacs, Potawatomis, Ojibwes, Delawares, Shawnees, and Great Lakes-area Iroquois, the Miamis wound up joining with the French. Around the time of the American Revolution and for years afterward, however, the Miamis sided with the British. Like many Native tribes, the Miamis felt the sting of encroachment onto Indian land by American colonists and settlers.

The first treaty between the Miamis and the United States government was the Treaty of Greenville, signed in 1795 following the Battle of Fallen Timbers. Following several victories over government forces by Chief Little Turtle, the Miamis were finally defeated by General Anthony Wayne at Fallen Timbers, marking the end of a period of Native resistance toward the taking of tribal lands without the consent of the inhabitants. In 1840, the Miamis signed another treaty under whose provisions they ceded tribal lands, in Indiana, to the United States. Under that treaty, the Miamis were moved out of Indiana to a reservation in what is today Miami County, Kansas. This move, from which only a select few Miamis were spared—mostly elected chiefs and mixed-blood tribal members—divided the Miamis into two groups, the Western Miamis and the Eastern Miamis. There was a good deal of movement between the two groups, and so many Miamis living in Kansas could claim ancestry with the Eastern Miamis.

Following the move to Kansas, many Miami people were stricken with disease and epidemic illness that caused the tribe to lose a great many members. Under the terms of the government's allotment act (which opened up Indian lands to individual ownership, first Native and then non-Native) and the federal removal policy, the Miamis again were moved, this time from Kansas into Indian Territory (present-day Oklahoma). Tribal members who wanted to stay in Kansas could do so only if they agreed to become citizens of Kansas; the rest were to become confederated with the Peorias and other nations in northeastern Oklahoma. This was one of the terms of the Treaty of 1867, the last treaty enacted between the United States and the Miamis.

Whether this confederation actually took place has been a matter of some debate. Many history books and land-allotment maps indicate that the confederation did occur, while scholars and other Native authorities maintain that it did not. Regardless of the extent to which this confederation took hold, at first the Miamis' move to Oklahoma seemed to further diminish whatever tribal autonomy they had enjoyed prior to their move to Kansas. Once in Indian Territory, the tribe came under the authority of various Indian agencies of the Bureau of Indian Affairs (BIA). By the time Oklahoma achieved statehood in 1907, the Miamis had been granted U.S. citizenship.

Before the move to Kansas under the 1840 treaty, the Miamis numbered more than one thousand. After the move and the onslaught of disease, those living within Kansas numbered only about three hundred. Agreeing to leave their land, which was already being settled by non-Indians, was the only way the small nation could survive. The Miamis of northeastern Oklahoma have long consisted mainly of mixed-bloods. Because of their small number, they really had no choice but to intermarry if they were to keep their Miami culture, history, and tradition alive.

In the years following their acquiring U.S. citizenship, the Miamis reorganized their tribal structure and have become quite sufficient in their governance. In the 1930s, the Miami Tribe of Oklahoma drafted a constitution, which was ratified by tribal members in 1939. In 1940, the tribe received a corporate charter, and in 1987, it amended its constitution. Although small in number, the Miamis maintain services for their citizens and keep their culture alive through language courses and their tribal library. Miami communities are tightly knit and hold several tribal events throughout the year to keep their citizens in touch with tribal business.

— S. S. Davis

SEE ALSO:
Dawes Commission; Fallen Timbers, Battle of; French and Indian War; General Allotment Act; Iroquois Confederacy; Oklahoma; Removal Act, Indian.

MICHIGAN

Michigan became the twenty-sixth U.S. state on January 26, 1837. The state's name comes from two Algonquian words: *michi*, which means "large," and *gami*, which means "lake."

There is a long history of Indians living in what is now the state of Michigan. Archaeological evidence indicates that Paleo-Indian hunters were in the area as long as ten thousand years ago. Michigan was also one of the many sites of the Hopewellian Mound Builder culture about twenty-five hundred years ago. At the time of first European contact, which took place in 1620 when Étienne Brulé visited Michigan's Upper Peninsula, Michigan was inhabited by four tribes. The Ojibwe, or Chippewa, people lived in the eastern part of the Upper Peninsula. The Ojibwes originally lived in many small bands that were independent of one another. The tribe developed a great deal of power through its connection with the fur trade, however, and formed tribal governance and tribal societies such as the Midewiwin, the Grand Medicine Society. The Ottawas, who derived their name from the Algonquian word for "traders," were located in the western part of the Lower Peninsula. They had been forced to move west because of pressure by the Iroquois Confederacy. The Potawatomis were located in the southwestern part of the Lower Peninsula, and the Wyandots, or Hurons, were in the southeastern part of the Lower Peninsula.

Two other tribes had once been in Michigan but had been driven westward. The Sauk, or Sac, people called themselves Osakiwuk, which means "people of the outlet." They were originally from the Saginaw Bay area in northern Michigan. During the 1600s, pressure from the Iroquois caused the tribe to move to the Green Bay area of Wisconsin. The Fox called themselves Meskwakihuk, meaning "Red Earth people." The tribe was originally from central Michigan, but they moved west into Wisconsin during the mid-1600s.

The first permanent European settlement in Michigan was founded in 1688 by Father Jacques Marquette at Sault Sainte Marie. During the late 1600s and the 1700s, the French, and later the English, carried out a great deal of fur-trading activities with Indian tribes in Michigan. Fort Michilimackinac was founded in 1715, and Mackinac was founded in 1780. (Both of these sites are reconstructed historical sites today.)

After the French and Indian War (1756–1763), the British gained control of Michigan. After the Revolutionary War, the United States took over Michigan, and it became part of the Northwest Territory. Indians in Michigan attempted to resist U.S. expansion into the region, but in 1794, the Battle of Fallen Timbers ended Indian resistance in the area. Indians gave up their lands in the southern part of the state and moved into remote regions of the northern Lower Peninsula and into the Upper Peninsula.

Seven reservations currently exist in Michigan. They are Bay Mills, Grand Traverse, Hannahville Community, Isabella, Lac Vieux Desert, Keweenaw, and Sault Sainte Marie. The reservations range in size from Isabella, which has 138,240 acres (55,296 hectares), to Grand Traverse, which has fewer than 100 acres (40 hectares).

The 1990 U.S. Census lists 55,638 Indians as Michigan residents, which ranks the state eleventh in terms of Native American population.

SEE ALSO:
Fallen Timbers, Battle of; Hopewell Culture; Iroquois Confederacy; Medicine Societies; Mound Builders; Ojibwe; Ottawa; Potawatomi; Wyandot (Huron).

MICMAC

The Micmacs have lived for centuries in the territory that currently makes up part of the Maritime Provinces of Canada. This area includes Nova Scotia, Prince Edward Island, eastern New Brunswick, and the Gaspé Peninsula of Quebec. The name *Micmac* means "allies" and helps explain the relationship among the various Micmac groups. Historically, their territory was divided into seven districts, but there was little political organization among the districts, and movement between districts was common. The Micmacs are from the Algonquian language group.

Before European contact, the Micmacs led a nomadic life based on the seasons, depending on hunting and fishing to supply their daily needs. During the winter, they hunted otter, beavers, moose, caribou, rabbits, and porcupines inland; during the summer, they fished for herring, salmon, and shellfish along the coast. Their material culture was centered on the cone-shaped houses called wigwams, which they covered with birch bark, woven mats, or evergreen boughs. They also used birch bark to build canoes. They made beautiful baskets and embroidered with porcupine quills.

Socially, the Micmacs were divided into households, local groups, and bands. The bands were headed by a chief, called a sagamore. Local groups gathered into bands only during the times of summer encampment along the coastal areas or during periods of war. Daily life of the Micmacs was dominated by a rich culture that included rituals for puberty, marriage, death, and the installation of chiefs.

A group of Micmac Indians pose with a Christian missionary outside a Native dwelling in nineteenth-century Nova Scotia. The coming of Europeans to eastern Canada initially meant an opportunity for the Micmacs to engage in trade and commerce. Over the years, however, the Micmac population was decimated by disease, and they were forced off their lands onto reserves.

Because of their location, the Micmacs were one of the first tribes contacted by Europeans, and from the beginning, they developed a liking for European trade goods. They became involved in the fur trade and were quick to accept the presence of Jesuit missionaries.

One result of this contact was a reduction in Micmac population due to disease. It is estimated that the Micmacs lost one-third of their population to typhus in 1746 alone, but over the years, they also fell victim to smallpox, dysentery, and alcoholism.

The Micmacs eventually lost much of their land, as well. With the end of the American Revolution, there was a sudden influx of Loyalists into eastern Canada. Some thirty-five thousand colonists moved to Nova Scotia alone; with these colonists came a demand for land. The British answer to this dilemma was to concentrate the Micmacs on reserves and make the rest of the land available to English settlers.

A Micmac participant at a Connecticut powwow. Dressed in traditional garb, he is demonstrating techniques of horse painting.

The reserve system, as well as the decline of the fur-trapping industry, changed Micmac life dramatically. While women and children stayed on reserves, the men often had to leave for periods of time to find work. They worked in the lumber industry and commercial fishing, were employed as guides, and found work as migrant farmworkers harvesting potato crops in Maine. Contemporary Micmacs have found high-paying work in the construction of high-rise buildings in the larger metropolitan areas of the northeastern United States and eastern Canada.

Those who stay behind on the reserves often face a life of poverty, unemployment, and alcoholism, although these are also the conditions of life for much of the non-Native rural Maritime Provinces as well. Conditions for the Micmacs are improving as the individual bands gain back more power from the central government and educational opportunities increase for tribal members.

The Micmac population has grown over the years. From population estimates at the time of European contact of between 5,000 to 6,000, the Micmacs have increased in number to 14,600 in Canada and another 2,700 in the United States during the 1990s. Those Micmacs who have remained in the Maritime Provinces are scattered on some twenty-seven reserves, with most in New Brunswick and Nova Scotia.

SEE ALSO:
Algonquian; Canada, Native–Non-Native Relations in; New Brunswick; Nova Scotia; Prince Edward Island.

MIGRATIONS, INDIAN, TO AMERICAS

SEE Beringia.

MILLS, BILLY (1938–)

Olympic gold-medal champion Billy Mills was born on the Pine Ridge Indian Reservation on June 30, 1938. In a stunning upset at the 1964 Olympic Games held in Tokyo, Japan, Mills won the 10,000-meter (10,900-yard) race. He had beaten such Olympic favorite runners as Ron Clarke of Australia and Mohammed Gammoudi of Tunisia. The United States had not won the race since 1912.

A tired but happy Billy Mills following his upset victory in the 10,000-meter run at the 1964 Tokyo Olympics.

A member of the Oglala Sioux Nation, Mills started to compete in track and field events at Haskell Institute, a government boarding school for American Indian students located in Lawrence, Kansas. At Haskell, Mills won the state 2-mile (3.2-kilometer) cross-country championship and the state mile (1.6-kilometer) title twice. His achievements won him a full athletic scholarship to the University of Kansas. There, he was named all-American three times and helped Kansas win the national track and field championships and the Big Eight Conference cross-country championship. In 1959, Mills represented the United States in the Pan American games held at Sao Paulo, Brazil.

After Mills graduated from Kansas, he joined the United States Marine Corps as a commissioned officer from 1962 to 1965. He competed in military track and field meets and won the interservice 10,000-meter (10,900-yard) run in Germany in 30:08 minutes. The marines sent him to the Olympic trials, where he qualified for the 10,000-meter run.

In 1972, Mills was named one of ten Outstanding Young Men in America. *Runners World* magazine voted his run as the most amazing upset in United States distance running.

Mills has a keen interest in young people and started an organization called Running Strong for American Indian Youth. The movie *Running Brave* documents his life and efforts that led to his Olympic championship. He was also named to the American Indian Athletic Hall of Fame. Mills now resides in Sacramento, California.

SEE ALSO:
American Indian Athletic Hall of Fame; Haskell Indian Nations University.

MINNESOTA

Minnesota became the thirty-second U.S. state on May 11, 1858. The state's name comes from a Sioux word that means "clouded water." American Indians have lived in what is now called Minnesota for thousands of years.

It is not clear when Europeans first visited Minnesota. According to some legends, Vikings pushed as far into the North American interior as Minnesota in the 1300s, but these legends have not been substantiated by archaeological evidence.

A family of Minnesota Ojibwes (Chippewas) at a maple-syrup camp in Cass Lake, Minnesota, in 1938. The Ojibwes, or Anishinabes, make up a large portion of the Native population of Minnesota.

Some supporters of the legends point out Norse-style "mooring holes" bored into rocks as evidence, but these features have not been verified as being authentic. French explorers such as Robert Cavelier, Sieur de La Salle; Samuel de Champlain; Daniel Greysolon, Sieur Duluth; Louis Hennepin; Jean Nicolet; and Pierre Esprit Radisson certainly explored Minnesota and had contact with Indians there during the 1600s.

The first permanent European settlement in Minnesota was Fort Anthony, which was built in 1819. At the time of this settlement, the major Native peoples who lived in Minnesota were the Santee Sioux, also known as the Eastern or Dakota Sioux; the Ojibwes, also known as Anishinabe or Chippewa; and the Cheyennes. Minnesota and northeastern Iowa were the homeland of the Santee people. The Ojibwes were originally from the Great Lakes area, but they had been forced west into Minnesota because of pressure from the Iroquois Confederacy. As the Ojibwes moved into Minnesota, they forced the Cheyenne people west onto the Great Plains. By the late 1600s, the Cheyennes had moved completely out of Minnesota.

Other eastern tribes briefly lived in Minnesota. The Hurons, or Wyandots, or Wendats as they called themselves, moved west into Wisconsin, Iowa, and Minnesota to avoid Iroquois attacks. The Omahas moved into Minnesota in the late 1600s but were forced out of the state and into Nebraska by the Santees. The Winnebago people were forced out of Wisconsin and into Minnesota in the mid-1600s by attacks from the Illinois, but they moved on to Nebraska by the early 1800s.

Only one brief period of Indian resistance to non-Native invasion took place in Minnesota. As more and more Europeans moved into the state, the Santee people entered into treaty agreements with the U.S. government. In 1862, the Santees rose up in revolt over the failure of the government to honor certain treaty agreements, resulting in Santee people dying of starvation. What began as a small conflict turned into widespread warfare, and after a few days, nearly five hundred European-Americans were killed. Horrible atrocities were carried out by both the Santees and the European-Americans during the short war.

As large numbers of troops poured into the state, the Santees surrendered. Over three hundred Santee men, almost all the Santee warriors who had surrendered, were sentenced to die for their part in the war. President Abraham Lincoln commuted the sentence of all but thirty-nine men. These men were all executed in a mass hanging, the largest mass execution ever held in the United States. The surviving Santees were moved to reservations in South Dakota and Nebraska, and Indian resistance in Minnesota ended.

Fourteen reservations exist in Minnesota today. They are Bois Forte, Deer Creek, Fond du Lac, Grand Portage, Leech Lake, Lower Sioux Community, Mille Lacs, Prairie Island Community, Red Lake, Sandy Lake, Shakopee, Upper Sioux Community, Vermillion Lake, and White Earth. Many of these reservations are very small, but Leech Lake has 677,099 acres (270,840 hectares) and Red Lake has 837,845 acres (335,138 hectares).

The 1990 U.S. Census lists 49,909 Indians as Minnesota residents, which ranks the state eleventh among states in Native American population.

SEE ALSO:
Illinois Confederacy; Iowa, State of; Nebraska; Ojibwe; Siouan Nations; Sioux Uprising (1862); Winnebago; Wisconsin; Wyandot (Huron).

MINOKA HILL, LILLIE ROSA (1876–1952)

Lillie Rosa Minoka was born on August 30, 1876, on the Mohawk St. Regis Reservation in New York. At age five, after the death of her parents, she was adopted by a Philadelphia physician, Dr. J. Allen. Her adoptive family enrolled her in the Grahame Institute, a Quaker boarding school for girls. When she was seventeen, she traveled to Quebec and Montreal, Canada, and converted to Catholicism.

Originally, she intended to become a nurse but was encouraged by her adoptive family to study medicine and become a physician. She returned to Philadelphia in 1894 and entered the Women's Medical College, only the second Native American to study there. In 1900, she was licensed to practice medicine and opened a busy practice with another woman physician. During those years, she met and fell in love with Charles Hill, an Oneida farmer from Wisconsin. She agreed to marry him, move to rural Wisconsin, and give up her medical practice.

The move to Wisconsin proved to be one of the most difficult adjustments of Hill's life. Not only had she been medically educated in the dominant society, she had no knowledge of the Oneida people. Committed to learning Oneida beliefs about disease and doctoring, she studied local herbs and combined their use with her existing medical knowledge. She became a trusted and reliable physician and friend to the Oneidas.

Between 1906 and 1915, Hill had six children. Shortly after the birth of her youngest, twin girls, her husband died of acute appendicitis. Refusing her Philadelphia friends' advice to return to the East, she cared for her children and her patients with the assistance of a trust fund from her adopted father's estate.

From the beginning of World War I to 1939, Hill was the only trained physician in the Oneida community. Without an official medical license in Wisconsin, she practiced from her home in what came to be known as her "kitchen clinic." She accepted little in cash payment and was gifted with as much food and supplies as her patients could manage. No one, Native or non-Native, was refused treatment for lack of payment. When Hill's trust fund collapsed with the 1929 stock market crash, her children convinced her to borrow the money to take the Wisconsin Medical License exam. With only four months to study, she passed the exam in 1934, thirty-five years after her graduation from medical school.

In 1946, at age sixty-nine, Hill suffered a heart attack, forcing her to limit her practice. However, her "kitchen clinic" remained busy until her death in 1952. Named "Outstanding American Indian of the Year" in 1947 by the Indian Council Organization, she was also honored with lifetime memberships in both the American Medical Association and the Wisconsin Medical Society. Her greatest honor, according to Hill, came in 1947, when she was adopted into the Oneida tribe. A memorial to L. Rosa Minoka Hill outside Oneida, Wisconsin, reads: "Physician, good samaritan, and friend to all religions in this community, erected to her memory by Indians and white people. 'I was sick and you visited me.' "

MISSION INDIANS

SEE California Missions; Missions for Indians, Christian.

MISSIONS FOR INDIANS, CHRISTIAN

The Native peoples of pre-Columbian America (that is, the Americas before the arrival of Christopher Columbus) had a deep respect for the land they inhabited. Native rituals and spirituality harkened back to a time when people lived in harmony with nature. They hunted primarily for subsistence purposes—food, clothing, and shelter. In some Native cultures, Father Sky cradled the sacred forces that blessed the trees, rocks, rivers, plants, and animals of Mother Earth. In their ceremonies and rites, Native peoples wore regalia and performed dances while impersonating animal spirits and other forces of the universe.

When the Europeans first encountered these Native rituals, they failed to recognize their profound spirituality. Driven by Christian religious fervor, white men saw Indians as savages practicing primitive paganism. The missionaries were priests and pastors from various Christian denominations who came to America along with the first conquistadores, trader-explorers, and other colonizing agents of Spain, England, France, and other European cultures. The primary goal of these missionaries was to spread the word of the Christian God throughout the Western Hemisphere.

At first, many Native Americans accepted Christianity, for Native religions welcomed new forms of worship, new powers, or medicine. But to the missionaries, Christianizing meant "civilizing" or instilling a new way of life, Since spirituality (what Europeans usually call "religion") was the foundation for all Native American social, political, and economic structures, the effects of European civilization on Native spirituality ultimately meant the destruction of other traditional Indian ways as well.

In order to save what they saw as the lost souls of Native Americans from eternal damnation, New England Puritans envisioned tightly organized set-

The Rancho de Taos Mission in Taos, New Mexico, was established by Spanish priests who belonged to the Franciscan order.

tlements called "praying towns," where Indians would live religious lives, praying, reading the scriptures, tending orchards or farming, grazing cattle, and learning such European crafts as weaving, baking, blacksmithing, leatherwork, and the manufacturing of olive oil, soap, or other goods.

In other areas, such as Florida, the Southwest, California, and French North America, Roman Catholic padres of the Dominican, Jesuit, Franciscan, and Augustinian orders oversaw the building of missions. By 1635, forty self-sufficient missions where Indians lived, worked, and worshiped separated from their traditional tribal ways existed in Florida alone.

Many of the padres used garrisoned soldiers to recruit recent converts or newly baptized Indians to fill schools where basic literacy and Bible studies were taught. Men and women were separated into different dormitories at night. Attendance at Mass was mandatory, and Natives who practiced their traditional customs were beaten. These types of missions spread into the Southwest, where Christianity was eventually integrated with traditional Indian ceremonies, and then farther west into California until 1833, when the Mexican government ended the Indian mission system.

In the Northeast, Jesuits accompanied trader-explorers like Père Marquette or Louis Jolliet down the Mississippi River during the mid-1600s. Jesuits often adjusted to Indian ways of life and even cared for the sick or counseled the troubled. Instead of settlements, missionaries of the northern region organized churches as well as day schools and, later, boarding schools for Indian children.

Initially, tribes like the Blackfeet were receptive to the Jesuits who preached and attempted to convert Natives. They found the gift of baptism useful as a strong medicine that protected warriors in battle. As tribal structure began to deteriorate during the fur trade and with the reduction of the buffalo herds in the late 1870s, Indian dependence on missions increased. Missions provided a needed center of social order and identity for Indians undergoing rapid social change.

The Protestants of the British colonies interpreted Indian depopulation from disease and famine as a sign that God intended the land for the English. They attempted to help the Indians by sending out Native converts or agents to preach salvation from alcohol and savagery.

These agents were so heavily engaged in ministerial roles that they failed to convert sizable congregations. During the eighteenth century and onward, however, Protestant missionary societies increased their efforts. They believed Native Americans could take on the substance of the Christian faith by accepting Euro-American civilization. Around 1880, the United States government set up government-owned Indian boarding schools to encourage acceptance of the Christian gospel, the Puritan work ethic, a sense of individuality, and economic independence.

Many Native healers and ceremonies were oppressed during the course of colonial mission building. Greatly weakened by disease and famine, many indigenous peoples concluded that evil was rampant because they were not allowed to perform their Native ceremonies; in some instances, Native people resisted the suppression of their beliefs. In 1675, for example, forty-seven Pueblo leaders of New Mexico accused of reviving Native religions were flogged. In 1680, one of these leaders, named Popé, organized a rebellion that drove the Spanish south into Mexico. Despite a Spanish comeback twelve years later, the rebel Pueblos managed to secretly maintain Native customs, combining them with the desirable Spanish introduction of wheat, fruit orchards, and livestock.

Oppression of the Shawnee prophet Tenskwatawa, who experienced visions that called for the rejection of all things European, helped to inspire Indian activism in the Great Lakes region. Yet a third healer, the Paiute prophet Wovoka, began the Ghost Dance in the late 1800s. This spiritual revival was meant to unite Indians with their dead ancestors and bind Indian-white culture through a sacred circle dance. It spread quickly among the Plains tribes. During the autumn of 1890, however, government agents ordered the Sioux to stop dancing. Some historical accounts claim the Ghost Dance died with religious leaders Sitting Bull and Big Foot at Wounded Knee. Wovoka, however, continued to heal through prayer until his death in 1932.

This cemetery is part of the San Xavier Mission in Tucson, Arizona. The impressive architecture and picturesque surroundings of many Spanish missions in the U.S. Southwest (once part of New Spain and then Mexico) belie the cruel methods that were often used to convert indigenous residents to Christianity.

A wall painting and icon depict the Virgin Mary at a mission church in New Mexico. By 1833, the government of Mexico (which then controlled most of the present-day U.S. Southwest) had ended the mission system. By 1848, New Mexico would be part of the United States.

Often the first whites to establish prolonged contact with Native Americans, missionaries introduced a whole new way of living to indigenous peoples. The traditional Blackfeet rhythm of life, for example, had consisted of the winter season, the spring hunting and root gathering, the summer hunting and Sun Dance when the entire tribe united, and the fall hunting and berry-gathering season. Instead, tribes were now encouraged to live sedentary farming lives, replace the extended family with a nuclear one, and abandon all traditional ceremonies for the one Christian God.

Some priests were like Bartolomé de las Casas, who in 1544 pleaded against Indian peonage (a system in which laborers are bound in servitude to their employers until certain debts have been paid off). In most cases, however, the missionaries advanced European cultural values, their interests converging with those of the settlers. In the name of civilization, for example, Christian reformers supported the General Allotment Act of 1887 and similar legislation aimed at policies expanding European-American interests, including the acquiring of territory through the breaking up of tribal land into individual allotments. As conflicts over land increased, so did misunderstandings, hostility, fraud, and injustice over treaties and agreements between two groups with such radically different cultures and worldviews. This conflict between cultures was characteristic of the entire period during which missionaries held influence over the lives and beliefs of Native peoples.

— K. Wedel

SEE ALSO:

Boarding Schools; California Missions; Catholic Church in the Spanish Empire; General Allotment Act; Ghost Dance Religion; Las Casas, Bartolomé de; Pueblo Revolt of 1680; Wounded Knee (1890).

MISSISSIPPI

Mississippi became the twentieth U.S. state on December 10, 1817. Archaeological evidence records Native peoples living in what is now called Mississippi thousands of years ago, and the state is known for its Mound Builder sites, including a historical Mound Builder site at Lake George–Holly Bluff.

Hernando de Soto, a Spaniard, was the first European to visit the region, in 1540. The first permanent European settlement was founded in 1699 by Pierre Le Moyne, Sieur d'Iberville, a Canadian-born French explorer who also founded many settlements in what is now Louisiana. At the time of first European contact, several Native tribes lived in Mississippi. The Chickasaw people lived in the northern part of the state, and the Choctaw people lived in the southern part of the state along with the Biloxi, Natchez, and Pascagoula peoples.

The Chickasaws were superb warriors who resisted de Soto's invading Spanish forces in 1541. They also fought against their Indian neighbors—the Cherokees, Choctaws, Creeks, and Shawnees. In 1729, they helped the Natchez in their fight against the French.

The Choctaws also resisted the European invasion of their land, but by 1837, both the Choctaws and Chickasaws were forced to give up their lands and move into Indian Territory in present-day Oklahoma.

One Indian reservation remains in Mississippi: the Mississippi Choctaw Reservation, which contains 17,926 acres (7,170 hectares) of land and has 3,932 Indian residents. The 1990 U.S. Census lists 8,525 Indian residents in Mississippi as a whole, ranking the state thirty-eighth in Native American population.

SEE ALSO:
Cherokee; Chickasaw; Choctaw; Creek; De Soto Expedition; Mound Builders; Removal Act, Indian; Shawnee.

MISSISSIPPIAN CULTURE

After 400 C.E., when the Hopewell mound-building culture entered its decline, there was a transition period of about four hundred years in the eastern woodlands before the rise of the next great cultural tradition, the Mississippian. This culture began to emerge by 800 C.E. and was still active, though it had entered into its decline, at the time Europeans arrived on the continent. The Mississippian was a culture known for the construction of temple mounds.

Important advances in agriculture, developed in Mexico and carried to the north by trade, are thought to have played a major role in the rise of Mississippian culture and its spread throughout much of the eastern woodlands. One of these was the development of new strains of corn that required a much shorter growing season. The earlier varieties of corn had required a growing season of about 200 days, which restricted their cultivation to people living in the southern parts of the eastern woodlands. The new varieties, however, could do well in areas that had growing seasons as short as 120 frost-free days, which allowed corn to play a vital role throughout the Mississippi River drainage system.

Perhaps of even more significance was the importing of Mexican beans, which occurred around 1000 C.E. Beans furnished protein, an item in the North American diet that had been supplied in the past largely by hunting game animals. Because of a lack of domesticated animals as a source of protein, this dietary deficiency had been a factor in restricting Native populations from concentrating in large urban centers. With the addition of beans as a cultivated crop, and with the new strains of corn to go along with squash, eastern woodland farmers had now put together the classic Native American agricultural package known as the Three Sisters (beans, corn, and squash). These crops complemented one another nutritionally and allowed Native agriculture to provide for the dietary needs of the population, which in turn allowed those populations to concentrate in much greater numbers than before.

The result was the development of the first true city in the eastern woodlands, Cahokia, near the Mississippi River in present-day southern Illinois. At its peak, around 1200 C.E., its population of about ten thousand was a rival of the cities of Europe of that era. Cahokia contained 120 mounds within a six-square-mile (sixteen-square-kilometer) area.

This ceremonial pipe depicts a figure with a carved feather mantle on its back wearing a headdress, earrings, and necklaces. Relics like this suggest the type of ceremonial regalia used by Mississippian mound-building peoples.

The largest of these, known as Monks Mound, has a base that is larger than the Great Pyramid in Egypt. The mound is a rectangle covering an area the size of thirty football fields. It is one hundred feet (thirty meters) high, containing 22 million cubic feet (616,000 cubic meters) of earth. It was constructed over a three-hundred-year period, in fourteen stages. A large wooden building stood on its summit.

Mississippian Culture is noted for constructing mounds that served as bases for elevated wooden buildings. Archaeologists have called these buildings temples, and Mississippian Culture is sometimes referred to as the Temple Culture. Each Mississippian community had at least one temple mound, and larger communities had many of them.

Mississippian Culture was widespread, and it varied somewhat by region. Middle Mississippian Culture was centered in what is today Tennessee and western Kentucky, and it encompassed portions of northwestern Georgia, the northern sections of Alabama and Mississippi, northeastern Arkansas, eastern Missouri, western and southern portions of Illinois, and southwestern Indiana. South Appalachian Mississippian Culture included most of Georgia and South Carolina and small portions of northern Florida, southeastern Alabama, and south-central North Carolina. Caddoan Mississippian Culture encompassed eastern Oklahoma, western Arkansas, northeastern Texas, and northwestern Louisiana. Plaquemine Mississippian encompassed a relatively small area in southwestern Arkansas, eastern Louisiana, and southwestern Mississippi, but it survived the longest. Its Natchez people were closely observed and described by the French in the early eighteenth century—and were also destroyed by them. A number of other Mississippian centers were active when the de Soto expedition passed through the Southeast in the 1540s, though the culture by then was in its decline.

Mississippian Culture concentrated in the rich bottom land within the floodplains of rivers. Even only slightly less desirable agricultural land was avoided in favor of these flood plains. This concentration of population may have been a key factor in the decline of the culture due to the rapid spread of indigenous Native diseases, especially tuberculosis, but also including disease associated with poor sanitation. Many centers had already been abandoned when the Spanish passed through in the 1540s. The Spanish also unleashed epidemics of European diseases for which the indigenous people had no immunity. By the time Europeans attempted to colonize the Mississippi River Valley, Mississippian Culture had disappeared nearly everywhere, leaving the mounds overgrown with grass and trees, except for its last remnant, the Natchez Nation.

—D. L. Birchfield

SEE ALSO:
Cahokia; De Soto Expedition; Epidemic Diseases; Hopewell Culture; Mound Builders.

MISSISSIPPI BAND OF CHOCTAW INDIANS

In the early 1830s, the Choctaws became the first Indian nation to be forced to move to new land west of the Mississippi River. Most of the Choctaws were removed to the West between 1831 and 1834, where they established a new Choctaw Nation on land that became known in 1834 as Indian Territory (present-day Oklahoma). However, Article XIV of the removal treaty of 1830, which is commonly known as the Treaty of Dancing Rabbit Creek, provided that any Choctaws who wished to remain in Mississippi and become citizens of the United States could do so. Article XIV also provided that each Choctaw head of household could choose 640 acres (256 hectares) of land in Mississippi, that Choctaw children above the age of ten could choose 320 acres (128 hectares), and that younger Choctaw children could choose 160 acres (64 hectares). Approximately six thousand Choctaws elected to remain in Mississippi. Many of them filed for landholdings under Article XIV, but the corrupt U.S. government officials who administered the treaty refused to process their claims. Only sixty-nine Choctaw heads of households were allowed to register for land in Mississippi.

The Choctaws who remained in Mississippi suddenly found themselves landless aliens in their ancestral homeland. Denied the rights of U.S. citizens, denied state citizenship, and denied the land due them under article XIV of the removal treaty, they lived on the margins of southern society for the remainder of the nineteenth century. Many of them took to the swamps in order to survive, where, ignored by the dominant Euro-American society, they lived by hunting and fishing with no land of their own, no schools, and no official recognition of their status as Indians.

At frequent intervals throughout the nineteenth century, delegations of Choctaws from the West visited the Mississippi Choctaws and tried to entice them to join the Choctaw Nation in the West. Many Mississippi Choctaws moved to the West during this period, but many also remained. In the West, the influences of a Choctaw school system and intermarriage with whites were producing rapid changes among the Choctaws, but in Mississippi, the isolated Choctaw communities were retaining both their language and their culture.

The United States government, for the most part, simply ignored the Mississippi Choctaws, until the U.S. Congress commissioned studies in 1908 and in 1916 to inquire into their condition. The studies revealed an appalling level of poverty. In 1918, the Bureau of Indian Affairs (BIA), working with an initial appropriation of seventy-five thousand dollars, established a Choctaw Indian Agency in Philadelphia, Mississippi. The BIA established schools in the Choctaw communities and began purchasing land for a Mississippi Choctaw reservation. By 1944, sixteen thousand acres (sixty-four hundred hectares) had been purchased.

In 1945, the Mississippi Choctaws were granted formal federal recognition by the U.S. secretary of the interior when they adopted a constitution and bylaws under the name of the Mississippi Band of Choctaw Indians. The constitution provided for the election of a tribal council, which then appointed a tribal chairman. In 1974, a revision of the constitution provided for the election of a chief for a four-year term.

In 1965, the Choctaw Housing Authority began constructing modern homes on the reservation. In 1969, the Chahta Development Company began constructing offices and buildings. A hospital with forty-three beds, the Choctaw Health Center, opened in 1976.

The construction of an industrial park in 1973 led to the establishment of manufacturing industries on the reservation. These include a division

U.S. artist George Catlin's likeness of Clermont, an Osage chief. The Osages were among the Native peoples living in the present-day state of Missouri at the time of French contact in the late 1600s.

of General Motors called the Chahta Wire Harness Enterprise, which assembles electrical components for cars; the Choctaw Electronics Enterprise, which makes car radio speakers; and the Choctaw Greeting Enterprise, which makes greeting cards for the American Greeting Corporation. These companies, and others, now provide jobs for more than one thousand Choctaws on the reservation.

Choctaws in Mississippi have retained their language and culture. The Choctaw language is still the first language in the home for more than 90 percent of the Mississippi Choctaws. Choctaw culture is celebrated annually for the benefit of visitors at the Choctaw Indian Fair, held each July at the reservation in Philadelphia, Mississippi. The weeklong event draws more than twenty thousand visitors each year and features the Stickball World Championship, traditional Choctaw food, pageants, and entertainment.

— D. L. Birchfield

SEE ALSO:
Bureau of Indian Affairs; Choctaw; Dancing Rabbit Creek, Treaty of; Five Civilized Tribes; Mississippi; Oklahoma; Removal Act, Indian.

MISSOURI

Missouri, which became the twenty-fourth U.S. state on August 10, 1821, takes its name from an Algonquian word meaning "big canoe people." American Indians have lived in the region that is now called Missouri for thousands of years.

The first Indians to live in the area were Paleo-Indian hunters of roughly ten thousand years ago. Later, the Mound Builder Culture was active in Missouri, and remains of Mound Builder sites can still be found throughout most of the state.

The first Europeans to visit Missouri were French explorers Father Jacques Marquette and Louis Jolliet, who traveled down the Mississippi River in 1673. The first permanent European settlement in Missouri was founded at Sainte Genevieve in the early 1740s. At the time of first European contact, four major tribes lived in the state: the Osages, the Sauks, the Foxes, and the Missouris.

As pressure grew from homesteaders moving into the state, the Indians of Missouri ceded their lands and moved to other regions.

No Indian reservations currently exist in the state, but the 1990 U.S. Census lists 19,835 Indians as residents of Missouri, ranking the state twenty-second among states in Native American population.

SEE ALSO:
Missouri Indians; Mound Builders; Osage; Sac and Fox.

MISSOURI INDIANS

The Neutache ("Those That Arrive at the Mouth") were called Missouri by Euro-American settlers. Over time, the tribe moved from present-day Wisconsin to Missouri. An argument between two Missouri chiefs caused a split among the tribe. One faction later known as the Otos went north. The other faction, the Missouris, stayed in the area of the Missouri River near the mouth of the Grand River.

The Missouris and the Otos speak Siouan languages of the Chiwere group. In the late 1600s and early 1700s, the Missouris established ties with the French and traded with them. In 1725, a French trader named De Bourgmont took several Missouris to France and presented them to Louis XV. They returned in 1727.

Disease and war with other tribes forced the Missouris to unite with the Otos. The two tribes made their first treaty with the United States on June 24, 1817. In the Treaty of Prairie du Chien, they ceded to the U.S. government all of their land east of Missouri up to the mouth of the Big Sioux River.

In 1854, the tribes ceded the remainder of their land except for a reservation along the Big Blue River on the present Kansas-Nebraska border. The reservation was later sold, and the tribes were moved to Indian Territory (present-day Oklahoma) between 1881 and 1882.

Today, the two tribes are known as the Otoe-Missouria Tribe of Oklahoma. Their tribal headquarters are located at Red Rock, Oklahoma, approximately twenty miles (thirty-two kilometers) south of Ponca City, Oklahoma. The tribe holds an annual encampment in July of each year.

SEE ALSO:
Missouri.

MITA

SEE Encomienda.

MIXTEC

At the time that the Toltecs and the Aztecs were the most important peoples in the Valley of Mex-

The columns rising above a patio on this ancient structure are characteristic of temples and palaces built by the Zapotec and Mixtec cultures from around 100 C.E. to 1500 C.E.

These women, descendants of the Mixtec peoples who once inhabited regions in southern Mexico, display items they have brought for sale at a market in the present state of Oaxaca.

ico, the Mixtecs developed societies near present-day Monte Albán in Oaxaca, a state in southern Mexico that borders the Pacific Ocean. The Mixtecs became well known for their "codices," colorful works of art in book form painted on animal hides that depicted Mixtec religious stories and royal genealogies from about 1000 C.E.

The artists who created the codices described epic stories of marriages, wars, and political intrigue (including murders) that, according to archaeologists Bruce E. Byland and John M. D. Pohl, "rivaled the works of Shakespeare and Sophocles." Another archaeologist, the Mexican Alfonso Caso, identified in the codices the life of a legendary king called Eight Deer and the existence of a major shrine called the Temple of Heaven. At this time, the Mixtecs built cities ruled by several royal families that were related to each other through intermarriage. Over the years, these families became quite large and formed factions that went to war with each other and destroyed much of the society that maintained their cities.

During their height, the Mixtecs were known as master artists and craftspeople. Their codices are some of the most spectacular artwork to survive the Spanish conquest. Before the arrival of the Spanish, the Aztecs often called Mixtec artists to Tenochtitlán to act as scribes of their own codices and to work in gold for them.

While the Mixtec codices are dazzling works of art, they are not historical works. Most of the stories they depicted described religious beliefs. According to Byland and Pohl, the codices reveal the Mixtec view of the world before the arrival of

Europeans: "The highest proportion of the surviving codices . . . deals with religious ideology, not history in the western sense."

See also:
Aztec; Maya; Mexico, Indigenous Peoples of; Olmec; Toltec.

MOCCASINS

Moccasin is an Algonquian word for footwear, but just as there are many Native nations, there are as many words to describe moccasins. There are also many distinctive styles of moccasins designed by the various nations and suited to the climates or terrains in which they live. Early European settlers soon learned that the soft-soled woodland moccasin was better than hard-soled shoes for travel in forests or in canoes and quickly adopted the moccasin as the most common form of footwear in colonial America. Moccasins were worn in every Euro-American family, winter and summer, and Native people often traded tanned deer and moose hides to cobblers to make moccasins within non-Native communities. Often, dog skins were tanned into a tough, durable leather for moccasins, and the term "putting on the dog" came to represent getting dressed up—that is, not going barefoot.

Moccasins in the Northeast were made of moose or deer and were often highly decorated with embroidered porcupine quillwork and later with beads. In the far North, hides were smoked to permeate them with oils and resins that protected the leather from snow and moisture. In the West, the

A display of moccasins featuring elegant beadwork graces the pages of a catalog issued by an art gallery in Santa Fe, New Mexico.

soles of moccasins were made of rawhide to guard against rocky terrain and as an aid when riding horses. The hard soles at the heels acted like spurs when controlling the horse with foot and leg pressure. In the Southwest, moccasins often had high tops to the knee, like boots, to protect against cacti. One form of Apache moccasin had a stiff rawhide toe panel that folded up so that cactus needles would not penetrate the soft toe leather.

There are also different styles of moccasin for men and women, and some nations had such distinctive sole shapes that tracks left on the earth revealed the nation or gender of the wearer. The decoration of moccasins was also very stylized by tribe and included the use of paint or ochres, beadwork patterns, fringes, tin cone jingles, or fur tails as drags at the heels. Many moccasins had fully beaded soles, and the myth arose that these were for funerals. Sole beading was merely another more elaborate art form often used in ceremony or on special occasions. However, among the Mohawks, funeral moccasins often had holes cut in the soles or pebbles inside to make the path uncomfortable so the spirit would not return to haunt the living.

SEE ALSO:
Beadwork and Beadworkers; Jewelry, Native; Quillwork and Quillworkers.

MOCTEZUMA

Moctezuma, or Montezuma (or, in the Aztec language, Motecuhzoma), was the leading figure in the Aztecs' political system early in the sixteenth century, when the homeland of the Aztecs was conquered by the Spanish under Hernán Cortés. Before Cortés arrived, Moctezuma had been plagued by terrible dreams in which he saw the Aztec Empire

In Tenochtitlán, the Aztecs' capital city, Aztec leader Moctezuma (also known in English as Montezuma) gives the Cortés expedition an elaborate diplomatic welcome to Mexico. This lithograph provides a representation of the lush surroundings that the Spanish conquistadores described in Tenochtitlán.

crumbling. Gone, he feared, would be the days of feasting when, after a battle, members of the ruling elite often hired musicians to memorialize the occasion in song. (A small orchestra usually played for Moctezuma at mealtimes as well. Most Aztec music had overtones not only of war and power, but also of divine rite. All ritual music was performed by members of a specially trained professional caste. An error, one small departure from the ritual, could result in death because an erring musician was said to disturb the gods. The rituals required well-developed memories, as well as a sense of creative showmanship.)

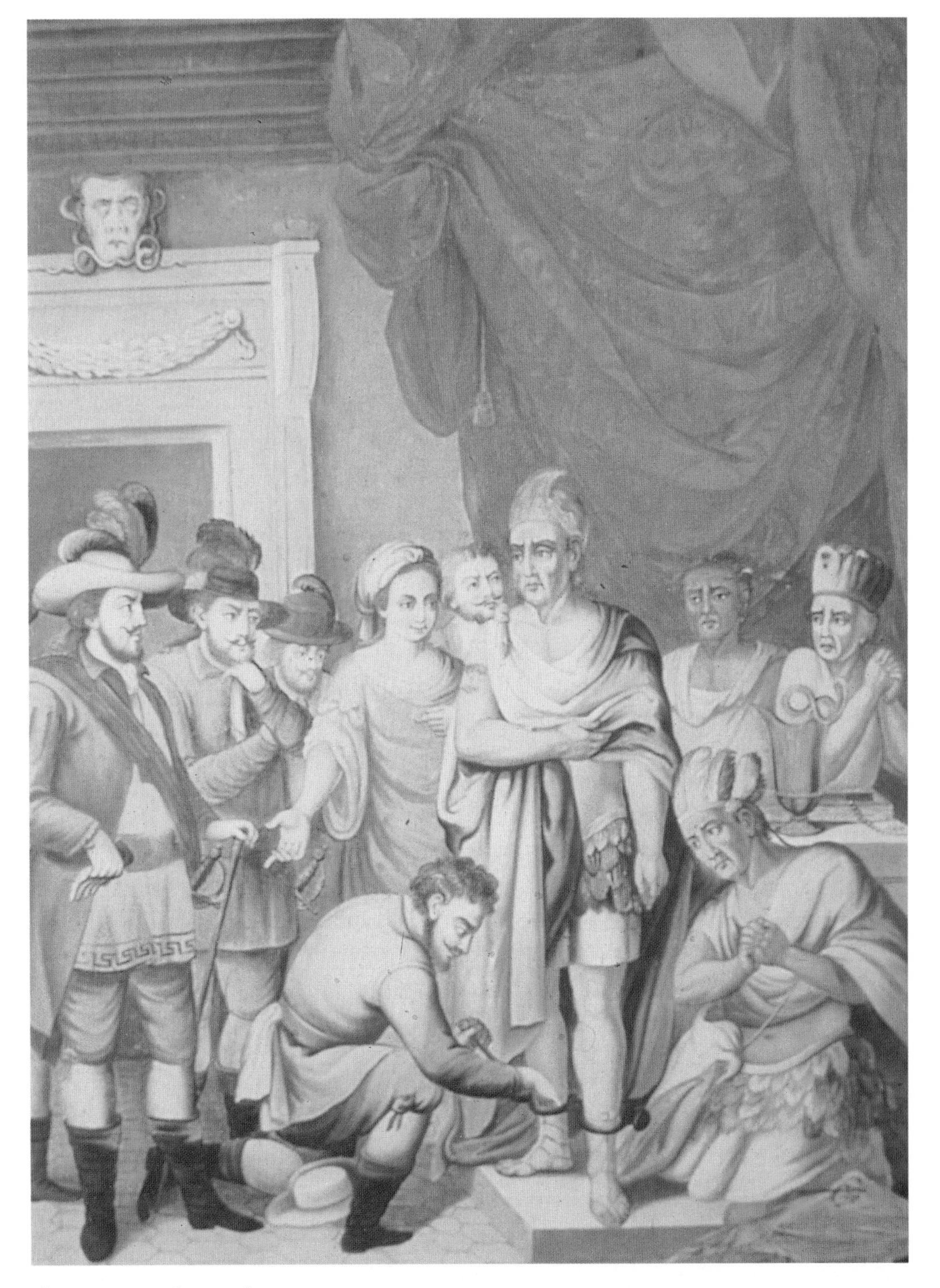

In this painting, Cortés is shown placing Moctezuma under arrest—the first step in the Spaniard's undermining of Moctezuma's power among his people. After months of imprisonment and torture, Moctezuma would perish at the hands of his captors.

Cortés and his allies were received in the Aztec capital, Tenochtitlán, as ambassadors of a mighty foreign nation. Moctezuma housed, fed, and entertained the men from Spain and gave them the run of the city. During this time, Cortés himself produced the written descriptions that today provide a glimpse of the city in its full flower. Cortés repaid hospitality with violence: At first, he took Moctezuma prisoner, then slowly, ruthlessly, undermined his power among the Aztecs. The imprisonment included physical and psychological torture.

The Spanish torture of Moctezuma was described by Benjamin Franklin. In November of 1774, following the Boston Tea Party, Franklin scoffed at proposals that Boston should negotiate a treaty with Britain while its port was closed and Boston was occupied by redcoats. "They will plead at ease, but we must plead in pain," Franklin argued. He compared Boston's position to that of Moctezuma in the hands of the conquistador Cortés, who demanded "a surrender of his cash." Franklin wrote that Moctezuma "made some objections and desired A TREATY on the reasonableness of the demand.

Kintpuash, better known to Anglo-Americans in California as Captain Jack. Faced with the loss of their lands and unbearable conditions on the Klamath Reservation, Kintpuash and several dozen fellow Modocs demanded a reservation of their own in 1870.

. . . Cortés heated a gridiron red hot, and seated poor Montezuma on it, and consented to TREAT with him as long as he pleased."

The Spaniards held Moctezuma captive for several months while rumors of his health spread through the capital. At one point, quite accidentally, Cortés's men discovered a massive amount of gold and silver that belonged to Moctezuma's father—in effect, the state treasury. The Spanish extracted 162,000 *pesos de oro* (19,600 troy ounces) of gold from him. At 1996 gold prices, this hoard would have been worth about $9 million. Most of the intricate artwork wrought from the gold was melted into bullion for shipment back to New Spain, although Cortés sent a few items intact to impress his sponsors with the quality of the civilization he had found.

After months of Spanish torment, Moctezuma was killed. The Spanish did their best to argue that he was struck in the head by a rock thrown by an outraged Aztec during a public speech. Díaz even says that the Spanish offered to feed Moctezuma and dress his wounds, but that he refused. The vague nature of his account indicates that Díaz was probably not an eyewitness to the murder. Cortés rather lamely excused himself by asserting that the murder occurred while he was away from Tenochtitlán, on his way back from the coast. The historical record indicates otherwise. Aztec sources, such as Chimalpahin, a native historian who based his work on the Aztecs' own codices (written history), argue that the Spaniards had strangled him.

SEE ALSO:
Aztec; Cortés, Hernán; Mexico, Indigenous Peoples of; Spain.

MODOC

The Modocs call themselves Maklak, meaning "people" in their Native language. The name *Modoc* comes from the Klamaths, who called them Moadok Maklaks, which means "people of the south." Both the Modocs and the Klamaths speak languages that come from the Lutuamian family.

The Modocs originated in California, where they lived in a "high desert" environment. They also traded widely with their neighbors to the south, east, and west. They also traded northward to the Columbia River area, participating in a big annual fair at Yainax. They were noticed by Spanish missionaries in the 1700s.

The Modocs signed a treaty with the United States government in 1854, ceding their lands in California, and were moved onto a reservation in Oregon with the Klamaths. The government refused to protect the Modocs from the Klamaths, who outnumbered the Modocs and refused to allow them to settle peacefully.

A band of Modocs led by Kintpuash, otherwise known as Captain Jack, left the reservation in 1870 and went to the Lost River, where they demanded a separate reservation for themselves. This caused the Modoc War of 1872–1873, when Captain Jack and about eighty warriors and their families retreated to the rocks and caves south of Tule Lake.

The Modocs knew that they would no longer exist if they continued to resist, so they surrendered. Captain Jack and other warriors who had participated in the resistance were hanged for an attack on members of a peace commission. (Two members of the commission, including General Edward R. S. Canby, died; one other member of the commission was wounded; and a fourth member escaped.) The rest of the Modocs were taken by train and military escort in 1873 to Nebraska, then on to Indian Territory in present-day Oklahoma, where they were given a reservation within the Eastern Shawnee Reservation. By 1890, all Modoc children of school age could read and write English, and they took great pride in attending school.

In the 1890s, allotments were forced upon the Modocs, as they had been forced on virtually every other tribal nation. Congress passed an act permitting those not wanting to remain in Indian Territory to return to the Klamath Reservation in Oregon, and by 1913, the last of Captain Jack's warriors had left Indian Territory and moved to the Oregon reservation. By 1948, the last full-blooded Modoc was also the only survivor of the Captain Jack band that had been forced into Indian Territory.

In 1954, the federal government scheduled the Klamath Reservation for termination, and although it became clear that many of the affected Indians did not fully understand the conditions or extent of termination, it was finalized in 1961. A 1974 court

Captain Jack (wearing a striped shirt), leader of the rebellion known as the Modoc War, and a group of Modoc warriors turned against U.S. participants in a peace conference, killing General Edward R. S. Canby and one other member of Canby's group. Captain Jack and several of his comrades were hanged for their role in the revolt.

case reaffirmed the hunting, fishing, and gathering rights of the Klamaths on former reservation land, however, and the Klamath Indian Restoration Act, passed on August 27, 1986, effectively restored federal recognition, rights, and privileges to both the Klamath and Modoc tribes. Today, though small in number, the Modocs have managed to keep alive their rich culture and traditions.

SEE ALSO:
Captain Jack (Kintpuash); General Allotment Act; Klamath; Modoc War; Termination Policy.

MODOC WAR

Before initial contact with the Spanish in 1769, Native American peoples in the area now called California were numerous and diverse. Hundreds of communities spoke distinctive languages and maintained unique cultures in geographical settings that varied from the mist-swept Northwest Coast to the searing deserts of the Southeast. Coastal populations began to fall after the Spanish subjugated many Indians in its mission system, which stretched from San Diego to San Francisco, and the Anglo-American invasion of the area following the discovery of gold in 1848 resulted in bloody warfare against Native Americans.

During the extermination of Native peoples in California, some Indians fought back. The Modoc Captain Jack (his Native name was Kintpuash) led a renegade band that rebelled against intolerable Klamath Reservation conditions in southern Oregon by taking to the northern California lava beds of their homeland. With about sixty compatriots, Captain Jack kept an army of up to a thousand soldiers at bay for seven months in the rugged country. He and his allies conducted warfare against the farmers in the Yreka area of northern California, and they kidnapped several non-Indian children.

Troops arrived in 1872 to force Captain Jack and his followers to return to the Klamath Reservation in Oregon. Before the army hanged him and three of his close friends, Captain Jack led a campaign through the lava beds of northern California that cost the lives of more than one hundred soldiers. At a peace conference, Captain Jack shot General Edward R. S. Canby, the leader of the non-Indian treaty commissioners, to death. Captain Jack often wore Canby's uniform from then to the day he was hanged. After the killing of Canby, the army shelled the lava beds with field guns to drive Captain Jack and his band out, effectively ending the resistance. Other Modocs were taken by train and military escort in 1873 to Nebraska and then were transported to Indian Territory (present-day Oklahoma), where they were made to live on a reservation within the Eastern Shawnee Reservation.

SEE ALSO:
California Indians; California Missions; Captain Jack (Kintpuash); Modoc.

MOGOLLON CULTURE

The Mogollon cultural tradition flourished in the Southwest from about 300 B.C.E. until about 1300 C.E. Centered in the Mogollon Mountains of southeastern Arizona and southwestern New Mexico, it extended into the Mexican state of Chihuahua.

The Mogollon tradition developed directly from the Cochise Culture, an Archaic period culture that had been developing in the region since the eighth century B.C.E. The Mogollon tradition developed at the same time as both the Anasazi and the Hohokam traditions, but the Mogollon shows little evidence of interaction with the other cultures until late in its history.

The Mogollon Culture appears to have been an egalitarian society throughout most of its history; there have been absolutely no signs of class distinction. No single village was more imposing than another, no house grander than another, and no burials have been discovered filled with luxury items. There is not even any evidence that the making of pottery was a specialization. In contrast, both the Hohokam and the Anasazi traditions offer ample evidence of a hierarchical society, one with people categorized according to their ability or status with a leader or leaders clearly in the top category. According to some scholars, this hierarchy was necessary in order to organize the labor for such projects as the Hohokam irrigation canals or the extensive Anasazi network of roads.

Mogollon pottery is unequaled by that of any other people of the Southwest during its time. It was the introduction of pottery that marked the end of the Cochise Culture and the beginning of the Mogollon tradition.

The most famous Mogollon pottery is called Mimbres. It was made in a cluster of villages along the Mimbres River in southwestern New Mexico between the eleventh and thirteenth centuries. Its distinctive black-on-white geometric decorations were painted with brushes made of shredded yucca leaves, brushes so delicate they could paint up to fifteen parallel lines within an area only three-quarters of an inch (about two centimeters) wide. Other Mimbres designs depict human, animal, insect, and mythological figures.

The ebb and flow of the Mogollon agricultural history has long baffled archaeologists. After many centuries of increasing dependence upon agriculture, the Mogollon people seem to have reverted to a hunting and gathering lifestyle between 500 C.E. and 700 C.E. This was followed by an intense period of increased farming and population expansion.

For most of their long history, the Mogollon people lived in pit houses in scattered settlements both in the mountains and in nearby valleys. Beginning about 900, Mogollon people began abandoning their pit houses and scattered settlements and began clustering in large aboveground stone pueblos. This development is thought to have been a result of Anasazi contact and influence. By 1250, Mogollon people had begun constructing cliff dwellings in the Anasazi manner. The Mogollon cliff dwellings at Gila Cliff Dwellings National Monument in New Mexico rival those of the Anasazi.

No one knows why the Mogollon tradition collapsed, but prolonged drought is thought to have been the main reason. By 1300, they had abandoned the region. Today, descendants of the Mogollon tradition are generally believed to be found among the Zuni, Hopi, Pima, and Papago (Tohono O'odham) peoples of the Southwest.

SEE ALSO:
Anasazi; Archaic Period; Arizona; Cliff Dwellings; Cochise Culture; Hohokam; Hopi; New Mexico; Pima; Tohono O'odham; Zuni.

MOHAWK

According to Edmund Wilson (in *Apologies to the Iroquois*), Mohawk is an Algonquian name for the enemies the Algonquians called "man-eaters." The people who are known as Mohawks call themselves "The People of the Flint." They are one of the five original nations of the Iroquois Confederacy (along with the Senecas, the Onondagas, the Cayugas, and the Oneidas). The confederacy, which played a pivotal role in colonial history, likened itself to a traditional Iroquois longhouse, in which the Senecas were said to live at the "Western Door" and the Mohawks at the "Eastern Door."

The Mohawks played an important role in the creation of the confederacy. Their oral history relates that both Deganawidah (the Peacemaker) and Hiawatha were adopted Mohawks and that the Mohawks were the first of the five nations to embrace a vision of peace and reason to end bloodshed. The Iroquois League was founded at an unknown date before sustained contact with European immigrants.

Mohawks have long played a central role in American popular literature, from James Fenimore Cooper's novel *The Last of the Mohicans* to popular Hollywood movies. A Mohawk disguise was adopted by colonists who participated in the Boston Tea Party.

Today, major Mohawk settlements include Akwesasne (or Saint Regis), which straddles New York State, Ontario, and Quebec at the Canadian–U.S. border near Massena, New York, and Cornwall, Ontario; Kahnawake, near Montreal; and Kanesatake, near the village of Oka, Quebec. The original homelands of the Mohawks covered much of northeastern New York State and areas of southern Quebec. Today, land claims have been filed for a small portion of that area. Some Mohawks also have established a community in the Mohawk Valley by purchasing private land.

During the early 1990s, several armed confrontations at all three reserves caused considerable controversy and violence. Two men—Matthew Pyke and "Junior" Edwards—were shot to death on May 1, 1990, at the peak of confrontations over smuggling and gambling.

The seeds of social disorder that gave rise to the controversy and violence were sown in Mohawk

In 1990, strife broke out among Mohawks over issues concerning tribal leadership. Here, a group on the St. Regis (Akwesasne) Reserve, which straddles the U.S.–Canadian border in New York, Ontario, and Quebec, form a procession at the funeral of Matthew Pyke, the first casualty of conflicts at St. Regis.

Country during the 1950s, with the construction of the Saint Lawrence Seaway. The Mohawks' homelands (and other areas) became sites for heavy industry and pollution. Since the 1960s, pollution has killed most farming at Akwesasne, and people may no longer eat fish or garden produce from the area. A General Motors toxic dump near Akwesasne is the most costly cleanup job on the Environmental Protection Agency's Superfund list of toxic sites.

After traditional means of making a living, such as fishing and farming, were destroyed by the seaway and resulting heavy industry, the geographical position of Akwesasne, straddling the U.S.-Canadian border, became a site of large-scale smuggling of alcohol and tobacco, as well as other drugs and weapons from the United States into Canada. A nationalistic Warrior Society was organized at Akwesasne, Kahnawake, and Kanesatake during the 1980s as a reaction to the poverty and brutality that often characterized life at all three reserves.

As traditional ways of life have become unworkable in Mohawk Country, many people have moved away, especially to urban areas such as Montreal and New York City. These are two of many metropolitan areas where Mohawks have become well known as builders of skyscrapers and bridges—the "Mohawks in High Steel," as they were called in the title of a memorable article by Joseph Mitchell in the *New Yorker* magazine.

In the midst of environmental contamination, smuggling, and gambling, a revival movement has begun taking place in Mohawk Country late in the twentieth century. The religion of Handsome Lake (called the Longhouse Religion in Mohawk Country) is as strong as it has ever been. Traditional Mohawks have established their own schools (such as the Akwesasne Freedom School) and museums (such as the Fadden family's Six Nations Iroquois Museum at Onchiota, New York). Today, at least a quarter of Mohawks are able to speak at least some of their native language, and the percentage has been rising.

— B. E. Johansen

Mohawk leaders who oppose tribal gaming and favor a traditional form of Mohawk governance discuss their views at talks in Montreal in 1990.

SEE ALSO:
Akwesasne Notes; Akwesasne (St. Regis Reservation), Pollution of; Brant, Joseph; Cooper, James Fenimore; Deganawidah; Gaming; Hendrick (Tiyanoga); Hiawatha; Iroquois Confederacy; Kahnawake Mohawks; Kenny, Maurice; Longhouse; Longhouse Religion; "Mohawks in High Steel"; Mohawk Warrior Society.

SUGGESTED READINGS:

Caduto, Michael J., and Joseph Bruchac. *Keepers of the Earth: Native American Stories and Environmental Activities for Children.* Golden, CO: Fulcrum, 1988.

Colden, Cadwallader. *The History of the Five Nations Depending on the Province of New York in America* [1727, 1747]. Ithaca, NY: Cornell University Press, 1958.

Grinde, Donald, Jr., and Bruce E. Johansen. *Exemplar of Liberty: Native America and the Evolution of Democracy.* Los Angeles: University of California, 1991.

Johansen, Bruce E. *Life and Death in Mohawk Country.* Golden, CO: North American Press/Fulcrum, 1993.

Morgan, Lewis Henry. *League of the Ho-de-no-sau-nee, or Iroquois* [1855]. New York: Corinth Books, 1962.

Tehanetorens [Ray Fadden]. *Tales of the Iroquois.* Rooseveltown, NY: *Akwesasne Notes,* 1976.

Wallace, Paul A. W. *The White Roots of Peace.* Santa Fe, NM: Clear Light Publishers, 1994.

Wilson, Edmund. *Apologies to the Iroquois, with A Study of the Mohawks in High Steel, by Joseph Mitchell.* New York: Farrar, Straus and Cudahy, 1960.

"MOHAWKS IN HIGH STEEL"

The destruction of the natural world, along with the erosion of the Mohawk land base, made living by the old Mohawk ways nearly impossible and prompted many to look for other ways to survive in the cash economy. During the first half of the twentieth century, some became the legendary "Mohawks in high steel," the men who constructed large parts of the urban skylines from Montreal to New York City.

The first Mohawks to work in "high steel" came from the Kahnawake Reserve near Montreal. In 1886, the Dominion Bridge Company, the largest builder of steel structures in Canada, erected a railroad bridge across the Saint Lawrence, which passed through the Kahnawake Reserve. The company agreed to hire Mohawks on the project. Later, Mohawks were hired to work on steel superstructures across Canada.

The work required athletic skills of climbing and balancing during heavy labor. It was dangerous for Mohawks and non-Indian workers alike; on August 29, 1907, the entire steel superstructure of the Quebec Bridge, nine miles (fourteen kilometers) from Quebec City, collapsed while it was under construction, killing ninety-six men, of whom thirty-five were Kahnawake Mohawks.

In 1915, a Kahnawake resident named John Diabo became the first Mohawk to work on the high steel of New York City. He got a job on the Hell Gate Bridge and was known as "Indian Joe." Diabo worked for a while on an Irish gang until several other Mohawks joined him, and then they formed their own working team. After a few months of work, Diabo, who was a superb athlete, slipped off a high beam, fell into the river below the bridge, and drowned. The rest of the work gang took his body back to Kahnawake and never returned.

A decade later, in 1925 and 1926, a large number of Mohawk steelworkers migrated to New York City, again because of a building boom of skyscrapers. Over the ensuing decades, the Mohawks became legendary as high-beam steelworkers in Manhattan, and their families established a community in Brooklyn in the Gowanus neighborhood. Their story was told in Joseph Mitchell's "Mohawks in High Steel," published in 1949 in the *New Yorker* magazine and later reprinted in Edmund Wilson's well-known *Apologies to the Iroquois*.

SEE ALSO:
Kahnawake Mohawks; Mohawk.

SUGGESTED READING:

Wilson, Edmund. *Apologies to the Iroquois, with A Study of the Mohawks in High Steel, by Joseph Mitchell*. New York: Farrar, Straus and Cudahy, 1960.

MOHAWK WARRIOR SOCIETY

According to John Mohawk, a professor of American Indian Studies at the State University of New York–Buffalo, the seeds of frustration among Mohawks and other Iroquois that gave rise to militant groups known as Warrior Societies were sown during the 1950s, when the governments of the United States and Canada ignored Native protests against construction of the Saint Lawrence Seaway. Mohawk, who is a Seneca, traces frustrations running from the first contact with Europeans intent on imposing their languages, cultures, and religions, as they took Native lands. During the 1950s, the ignoring of Native complaints about the seaway fit into an official policy of "termination," by which Native reservations were to be broken down as Indians were absorbed into the "American mainstream" in both the United States and Canada.

In 1990, Mohawk Country was hit by strife. The disputes and turmoil that paralyzed Mohawk Country were not a series of isolated events, but the violent culmination of the many events and issues that had grown out of the ruination of the traditional way of life. The nationalistic, military-like Warrior Society, which played a key role in the strife, might never have arisen without construction of the Saint Lawrence Seaway shortly after World War II. Construction of the seaway and industrialization of the area destroyed traditional ways of making a living in Mohawk Country. Gambling and smuggling then emerged as ways to make money, sometimes under Warrior Society claims of "sovereignty," or independence as a Native nation.

During 1990, the events in Mohawk Country were accompanied by a rising, often emotional, debate over the future of the Iroquois Confederacy as a whole. At the heart of this debate were two interpretations of Mohawk history and tribal governance. One interpretation belonged to the Iroquois Grand Council at Onondaga (in New York State), the Mohawk Nation Council, and many of the other national councils that make up the Iroquois' original political structure. These people oppose violence and look at the Warriors as illegitimate. The other interpretation, espoused by the Warriors (synthesized by Louis Hall, a Kahnawake Mohawk and the Warrior Society's founder), rejects the governing tribal structure as a creation of white-influenced religion (especially the Quakers) and advocates a revolution from within to overthrow it.

Francis Boots, a leader of the Mohawk Warrior Society, which opposed traditional forms of tribal governance and favored tribal gaming as a way of making money, at a conference discussing the standoff between Mohawk factions at three reservations in 1990.

Hall's manifesto, *Rebuilding the Iroquois Confederacy*, claims that the Warriors hold the true heritage of the Iroquois and that today's traditional council and chiefs at Akwesasne have sold out to elitism, the Quakers, Handsome Lake, and white interests in general. In the manifesto, Hall regards the Code of Handsome Lake (called the Longhouse Religion) as a bastardized form of Christianity grafted onto Native traditions and regards its followers, including many gambling opponents, as traitors or "Tontos." Handsome Lake's visions are called the hallucinations of a drunk. (The Code of Handsome Lake began as a series of visions in 1799 and combines European religious influences, especially those practiced by the Quakers, with a traditional Iroquois emphasis on family, community, and the centrality of the land to the maintenance of culture.)

During the heat of the dispute over tribal governance and the direction of the Iroquois Confederacy, the arguments led to heated, often violent debate. According to Hall and his followers, any Iroquois who did not subscribe to his ideology was a racial traitor in his eyes, a sellout to Handsome Lake and the Quakers. At one point, Hall argued in favor of mob-style "hits," or executions, of many of the Iroquois chiefs (including the entire Onondaga council) for following the peace-oriented path. In 1991, shortly before his death, Hall withdrew the death threats and said that the Warriors would work to replace the sitting grand council by peaceful means.

SEE ALSO:
Hall, Louis; Handsome Lake; Iroquois Confederacy; Kahnawake Mohawks; Longhouse Religion; Mohawk.

MOIETIES

Many Native American tribes are divided into two groups. Though the names of the groups vary from tribe to tribe, anthropologists call such groups "moieties." Tribal names for the two moieties, or groups, in the tribe usually refer to opposing principles or qualities. The most commonly used names translate into the English words *peace* and *war*. Other common pairs of group names are "black" and "white," "summer" and "winter," and "elder brother" and "younger brother." Often, more than one name may be applied to a single group. Depending on circumstances, for example, one moiety in a tribe might be referred to as the Peace, Elder Brother, or Summer group. In every instance, each of the names that tribal members apply to a single group is thought to be naturally related or connected in some way.

Moieties serve many important roles. In virtually every case, moieties are exogamous, meaning that people must marry outside their moiety. Requiring that people marry outside their own narrow group ensures good genetic health by keeping the gene pool as large and diverse as possible. Marrying outside of one's moiety also helps maintain social harmony among the various elements of the tribe. People feel loyalty to their own moiety, but because they are married to someone of the opposite moiety, they are thus related to the opposite moiety. Moieties also help promote social harmony by ensuring that communal responsibilities are divided between the moieties. In tribes that have peace and war moieties, for example, a chief from the peace group will usually be the leader in times of peace, and a chief from the War group will lead during conflicts. Many other responsibilities are divided as well. In some tribes, each moiety takes on the duty of burying the dead of the other moiety.

Pulitzer Prize-winning author N. Scott Momaday addressing the United Nations General Assembly in New York City in November 1993 for the Cry of the Earth Conference.

Membership in a moiety is generally determined by descent. In most tribes, the line of descent is matrilineal, meaning that children are members of their mother's moiety. In a few instances, it is patrilineal—that is, determined by the father's membership. In any case, moiety membership is one of the most important factors in the identity of a person born into his or her moiety, just as belonging to a family helps determine a person's sense of personal identity.

The importance of moieties has greatly diminished in recent history, although understanding such groups is still central to understanding the social and political order of tribes such as those in the Iroquois Confederacy.

SEE ALSO:
Iroquois Confederacy; Philosophy, Native.

MOMADAY, N. SCOTT (1934–)

Poet, novelist, essayist, artist, and member of the Kiowa tribe, N. Scott Momaday was born in Oklahoma. He spent much of his childhood living on Indian reservations in the Southwest and considers northern New Mexico his spiritual home. After high school, he graduated from the University of Arizona and holds master's and Ph.D. degrees from

Stanford University. After graduating, he spent several years teaching in California, both at Stanford and at Berkeley.

Scott Momaday is without question one of the most important Native American writers. He has been writing for nearly thirty years and won the Pulitzer Prize for literature in 1969 for his book, *House Made of Dawn*. No other American Indian has won this prestigious award.

His other books include *The Ancient Child, The Names, The Gourd Dancer, Angle of Geese and Other Poems*, and *The Way to Rainy Mountain*, which tells the story of the migration of his Kiowa ancestors from northern Montana to the Southern Plains. For his lasting contributions to literature, he received the Native American Lifetime Achievement Award in 1992 and the Premio Letterario Internazionale "Mondello" Award, a prize given to writers of international repute.

Besides writing poetry, novels, plays, and short stories, Momaday is also a painter. Some of his paintings have been exhibited in the United States and in Europe. The father of three daughters, he currently lives in Tucson, Arizona, with his wife, Reina, and his daughter Lore, where he is a professor of English at the University of Arizona.

MONEY

SEE Indian Giver; Wampum.

MONTAGNAIS-NASKAPI

In historic times, the Montagnais-Naskapi Indians occupied the greater part of the Labrador peninsula in eastern Canada. This territory encompasses parts of the present-day provinces of Quebec and Newfoundland. The designation of Montagnais-Naskapi represents a threefold division of this territory. The Naskapis lived in the north, the Montagnais in the south, and the East Crees in the west. All of these groups spoke dialects of Eastern Cree, a part of the Algonquian language group.

The historic Montagnais-Naskapis subsisted primarily by hunting. They used the bow and arrow to hunt larger game like caribou and moose, snares to catch smaller game, and nets to catch beaver and otter. With the arrival of the Europeans, many of the Montagnais-Naskapis traded furs. The most common form of housing was a conical-shaped lodge, and caribou hide was used for clothing. They were a mobile people whose transportation needs were met by canoes in the summer and toboggans and snowshoes in the winter. The basic socioeconomic group was of three to four families and from fifteen to twenty people. Several bands would stay in close proximity during the winter months.

Because the land they occupied was not immediately desirable to Europeans, the Montagnais-Naskapis were able to maintain their traditional lifestyle into the twentieth century. As land became more valuable and as game became depleted, however, the Montagnais-Naskapis have been forced into a more sedentary life. This transition in lifestyle has had a severe psychological impact on bands as they see their old way of life disappear.

In recent years, the Montagnais-Naskapis have come to be known as the Innus. The Innu Nation, an organization representing political and cultural interests of the Montagnais-Naskapis in Labrador, was created in 1990. Currently, there are about eighteen Innu bands on the Labrador peninsula. In 1991, their population was 12,045.

SEE ALSO:
Algonquian; Newfoundland; Quebec.

MONTANA

Montana became the forty-first U.S. state on November 8, 1889. Montana, whose name comes from a Spanish word that means "mountainous region," has a long history of Indians living within the region. Early Paleo-Indian hunters were in the area thousands of years ago.

During the 1700s, pressure from East Coast tribes forced groups such as the Cheyennes, Crows, and Sioux westward into the area of present-day Montana. Tribes that already lived in the region—such as the Flatheads, the Shoshones, and the Kutenais—were forced farther west into the mountains of far western Montana. Therefore, when the first

A young member of the Crow tribe in traditional attire for an event at the Crow Reservation in Montana.

Europeans, members of the Lewis and Clark party, visited the region in 1805, they met many different groups of Indians.

The first permanent European settlement was founded in 1841, when Belgian-born missionary Pierre Jean De Smet established Saint Mary's Mission. In the late 1850s and early 1860s, gold was discovered in Montana. The 1860s also saw the start of the Montana cattle industry when Texas cattlemen brought the first herds into the region.

The Sioux and Cheyenne tribes resisted the invasion of their lands. This resistance reached its high point in 1876, when Lt. Colonel George Armstrong Custer's force of soldiers was beaten at the Battle of the Little Bighorn. (The Little Bighorn Battlefield, near Billings, is now a National Monument.) The Sioux and Cheyenne resistance ended soon after the battle, but Indian resistance resurfaced in Montana in 1877, when Chief Joseph and his Nez Perce band left their reservation and attempted to reach freedom in Canada. (The Chief Joseph Battlefield State Monument commemorates the site of the great chief's surrender.)

Seven reservations are currently in Montana. They are the Blackfeet Reservation, the Crow Reservation, the Fort Belknap Reservation, the Fort Peck Reservation, Rocky Boy's Reservation, and the Northern Cheyenne Reservation.

The 1990 U.S. Census lists 47,679 Indians as Montana residents, placing the state twelfth among U.S. states in Native American population.

SEE ALSO:
Blackfeet; Cheyenne; Chief Joseph; Crow; Lewis and Clark Expedition; Little Bighorn, Battle of the; Nez Perce; Ojibwe; Shoshone; Siouan Nations.

MONTEZUMA, CARLOS (1866?–1923)

Physician and Indian-rights activist Carlos Montezuma (also known as Wassaja) was born in south-central Arizona to Yavapai parents sometime in the mid-1860s. He was captured during a raid by Pima Indians in 1871 and was later sold to prospector and photographer Charles Gentile for thirty dollars. Gentile had his young charge christened Carlos Montezuma in November of 1871. In 1877,

An undated photo, probably from the late 1800s, of a group of Crow children playing hockey in a field outside their school in Montana.

Mormon leader Brigham Young (shown pointing) and a group of Mormon followers in Shoshone Country on the shore of the Great Salt Lake. Their settlement would become Salt Lake City, Utah.

dence, most of them moved again to a new settlement in Nauvoo, Illinois. Local non-Mormons around Nauvoo were no friendlier than in Independence, and as Mormons became the dominant group in their new area, mobs gathered and burned their homes and businesses.

In the midst of all this, in 1844, Smith decided to counter anti-Mormon biases by running for president of the United States. His plans were never realized, however, because on June 27, 1844, Smith was murdered by an anti-Mormon mob. After burying him, the Mormons moved out of Illinois, journeying westward, looking for their "promised land," under the leadership of Brigham Young.

As they crossed the Missouri River from Iowa to Nebraska during the mid-1840s, the Mormons entered Indian Country. They were respectful of the Native peoples, believing that they had a common biblical heritage. The Mormons usually negotiated with Indians before entering their lands and maintained amiable relationships with them as they traveled. With the permission of the Omahas and other Native peoples in eastern Nebraska, the Mormons erected a winter camp on the site that would become the city of Omaha ten years later.

In the late 1840s, a large party of Mormons under Brigham Young settled on the southern edge of the Shoshone homeland at the Great Salt Lake. It was here that the Mormons established the beginnings of a settlement, which they called Deseret, that would lead to the founding of the state of Utah. In 1851, the Shoshone chief Washakie allied for a time with the Mormons, before the federal government asserted authority over the religious group as part of Utah's bid for statehood. In 1857, President Buchanan ordered about twenty-five hundred U.S. troops into Utah to suppress a large-scale Mormon rebellion against U.S. authority. This rebellion was led by a group of Mormons who called themselves the Danites, or Avenging Angels, and advocated murder and other acts of revenge against U.S. officials.

Before the army could reach Utah, a dispute broke out between some Mormons and a group of Missouri settlers over the Mormons' refusal to sell supplies to the settlers. A series of minor altercations took place between the Missouri migrants and the local Mormons, and when the newcomers started roughing up a group of local Indians, some Mormons seized the opportunity to fan the flames of anger between the Missourians and the Indians. When the Indians fought back against the attacks by the Missourians, a Mormon leader, on the pretext of acting as a negotiator, persuaded the Missouri settlers to surrender their arms in exchange for a promise by the Indians to let them leave. When the Missourians laid down their arms, a group of Mormons and Indians slaughtered the adults in the group—120 by some counts—and the Mormons adopted into their community the 17 small children they had spared.

The Mormons reportedly attempted unsuccessfully to hide their instigation of what came to be known as the Mountain Meadows Massacre and lay the entire blame on the Indians. By the time the army arrived, the Mormons had softened their stand on certain issues regarding religious and political independence, and for years Mormon residents and U.S. Army soldiers stationed in Utah became virtual trading partners, at least until the military presence in Utah was reduced in 1860–1861 at the outbreak of the U.S. Civil War. Deseret, as Utah continued to be called by its Mormon inhabitants, finally became a U.S. state in 1896 following the Mormons' formal renouncing of polygamy in 1890. Today, the Church of Jesus Christ of Latter-day Saints continues to exert a dominant influence on the politics, character, and demographics of Utah, with Mormons making up about two-thirds of its population.

— B. E. Johansen

SEE ALSO:
Nebraska; Omaha; Utah.

MORTALITY RATE

Mortality rates provide a statistical portrait of people's deaths from all causes and place them in order of leading causes. In the case of Native Americans, mortality rates may vary according to geography, the reliability of the methods of reporting, and the conditions under which various Native groups live.

The mortality rate for non-Indians in the United States in the years 1989 to 1991 was 520.2 per every 100,000 people. According to statistics kept by the twelve regional offices of the Indian Health Service (IHS), however, the mortality rate for Indians—as recognized by the federal government—during that same time was 585.2 per every 100,000 people. Three districts—Oklahoma, Portland, and California—have problems with underreporting on the Indian population, so many Indians are not listed as such on death certificates. (These districts also have many Native-run health clinics or IHS hospitals.) When those three areas are excluded from IHS statistics, the mortality rate of Indians jumps to 713.9 deaths per 100,000 people. However, the Aberdeen district of the Great Plains had 1,067.2 deaths per every 100,000 people, more than double that of the U.S. national average.

Years of Productive Life Lost, an indicator of premature deaths, is defined as deaths of people under the age of sixty-five. The years of productive life lost for all races of the United States was 56.2 per every 1,000 people in the years 1989 to 1991. But for the Indian population, it was 86.7 per every 1,000 people. When the three underreported areas were excluded, the rate was 109.2 per every 1,000 people. Again, the Aberdeen district topped the scale with the rate of 147 per 1,000 people under the age of sixty-five.

The leading cause of death for all races and for the Indians was diseases of the heart, although some districts had other causes. For Indians, however, the second leading cause of death was accidents and adverse effects of certain living conditions. In the Alaska, Albuquerque, and Navajo districts, accidents and adverse effects were the leading cause of death.

Indian youths between the ages of fourteen and twenty-five years have a death rate of 239 per 100,000 population, while non-Indians have a death rate of 99 per every 100,000. One of the leading causes of death for young Indians was automobile accidents, which accounted for 98 deaths per 100,000 people. Other accidents accounted for 39 deaths of every 100,000 in the fourteen- to twenty-five-year-old category. Only 38 of every 100,000 non-Indian people died in auto accidents, and only 11 per every 100,000 died from other accidents. While 36 Indians of every 100,000 died from sui-

An 1899 photo of an orchestra made up of Native students at the Hampton Institute, Virginia, which specialized in providing training programs for American Indians and African-Americans. One objective of these programs was to boost Native Americans' education and job prospects, two factors that may affect the quality and length of life for Indian people. But programs such as these often made life even more difficult for returning Indians trying to readjust to life in their Native communities.

cide, about 13 of every 100,000 non-Indians took their own lives. And 29 per 100,000 Indians died because of homicide as compared to 14 of every 100,000 non-Indians.

According to the IHS division director of clinical and prevention services, the reasons for the high mortality rate among Indians are complex. The dynamics of what Indians face in the United States contributes to behavior that is risky and often self-destructive. People with less sense of the future take more risks, thus engaging in behavior that adds to the mortality rate.

A number of factors, such as lower education levels and prospects for employment, may combine to produce lowered expectations for the future. For example, only 65.3 percent of the Indian population has a high school diploma, while 75.2 percent of the non-Indian population has graduated from high school. The trend continues in postsecondary education; 9 percent of the Indian population has a bachelor's degree or higher, while 20.3 percent of the non-Indian population has a bachelor's degree or higher. More disturbing is the unemployment rate for Indians. Non-Indians have an unemployment rate of 6.4 percent for males and 6.2 percent for females. Among Indians, the unemployment rate is 16.2 percent for males and 13.5 percent for females. Some areas where the mortality rate is higher have proven to be areas where the Indian population has a higher unemployment rate and a greater number of people living below the poverty level.

In addition to these factors, the median household income for Indians is two times lower than the income for non-Indians. And while 13.1 percent of the non-Indian population is living below the poverty level, 31.6 percent of all Indians are living below the poverty level. In IHS districts with higher numbers of suicide, homicide, and alcohol-related deaths, the percentage of Indians living below the poverty level is above 40 percent. Within the Aberdeen district, almost 50 percent of the people live below the poverty level. In the years 1989 to 1991, 51.8 deaths per every 100,000 were related to alcohol among the Indian population, while only 7.1 deaths per every 100,000 population was alcohol-related among other races in the United States. In the Aberdeen district, where poverty and unemployment are so high, the alcohol-related deaths reached 95.6 per every 100,000 population.

According to IHS officials, many Indians are faced with a no-win situation. With fewer job opportunities on the reservations or in heavily populated Indian communities, those with higher educations must leave their culture to obtain money; their only other choice is staying in their communities where there are no jobs. Although tribal leaders from all Indian nations are trying to change these statistics by creating broader economic bases, the statistics for Indian people are still grim.

— S. S. Davis

SEE ALSO:
Infant Death Rate.

MOTHER EARTH

The Native peoples of North America lived in roughly two thousand distinct societies and spoke several hundred mutually unintelligible languages at the time of first sustained contact with Europeans. However, these diverse cultures all shared ways of life that involved an intimate connection with the natural world.

Indian scholar Vine Deloria, Jr., suggests that the natural metaphor of earth as mother can be documented by non-Natives as far back as 1776. On June 21 of that year, at a conference in Pittsburgh during the Revolutionary War, Cornstalk, who was trying to convince the Mingos [Iroquois] to ally with the American colonists against the British, said, "All our white brethren . . . have grown out of this same ground with ourselves[,] for this Big [Turtle] Island being our common Mother, we and they are like one Flesh and Blood."

This girl, photographed in 1995 at the Kitigan Zibi school in Maniwaki, Quebec, benefits from an education that is aimed at using the language and other characteristics of her culture as tools of learning. A good education—one that helps people gain better employment while keeping their cultural ties strong—is a key to giving Indian children a brighter and longer future.

A Navajo pot created by contemporary potter Lucy McElvey combines the images of Father Sky and Mother Earth. Despite the enormous diversity in languages and cultural beliefs among the hundreds of Native American societies, most Indian cultures have held to the idea that humans have a personal connection with the natural world.

rofessor of anthropology,
Native Americans had an
'pan-Indian mythology"
environmentalists in the
orical record is full of ref-
' by Native people. Black
ation near Fort Madison,
h war that bears his name,
address to a mainly non-Indian audience in the late 1830s by observing, "The Earth is our mother; we are on it, with the Great Spirit above us."

In 1877, the Nez Perce chief Joseph replied to an Indian agent's proposal that he and his people move to a reservation and become farmers. This statement was made a few months before Joseph and his band fled 1,700 miles (2,737 kilometers) across some of the most rugged land in North America to avoid subjugation. Chief Joseph said, "The land is our mother. . . . She should not be disturbed by hoe or plow. We want only to subsist on what she freely gives us." Smohalla, a religious leader of the Nez Perce, said at the same meeting, "You ask me to plow the ground? I should take a knife and tear my mother's bosom? Then when I die, she will not take me to her bosom to rest. . . . You ask me to dig for stone! Shall I dig under her skin for her bones? Then when I die I cannot enter her body to be born again. You ask me to cut grass and make hay and sell it, to be rich like white men! But how dare I cut off my mother's hair?" A third Nez Perce chief, Tuhulkutsut, joined in, "The earth is part of my body. I belong to the land out of which I came. The earth is my mother."

United States negotiator General Oliver O. Howard then is recorded to have protested, "Twenty times over [you] repeat that the earth is your mother. . . . Let us hear it no more, but come to business." The Lakota holy man Black Elk told John Neihardt that "every step that we take upon You [the earth] should be done in a sacred manner; every step should be taken as a prayer."

Ecological metaphors also were woven into the languages of many Native American cultures. "Who cuts the trees as he pleases cuts short his own life," said the Mayas. In fact, the Maya word for "tree sap" is the same as the word for "blood."

Authors Christopher Vecsey and Robert W. Venables argue that many Native cultures across the continent share concepts characterizing the earth as sustainer (or "mother") and the sky as "father," realm of the Creator, or "Great Mystery." They also trace the use of the concept of the "sacred circle" (or "hoop") as a metaphor for physical and spiritual unity: "The American Indians' concept of a sacred circle expresses a physical and spiritual unity. This circle of life is interpreted according to the particular beliefs of each Indian nation, but is broadly symbolic of an encompassing creation." One of the themes of their work is the conflict that occurs when the Indian nations, who saw their environments as sacred and interdependent with them, confront waves of Europeans and European-Americans "who saw in the environment a natural resource ordained by God for their sole benefit."

— B. E. Johansen

SEE ALSO:
Black Elk; Black Hawk; Chief Joseph; Chief Seattle; Howard, Oliver O.; Neihardt, John.

SUGGESTED READING:
Awiakta, Marilou. *Selu: Seeking the Corn-Mother's Wisdom*. Golden, CO: Fulcrum Publishing, 1993.

MOUND BUILDERS

Throughout the eastern woodlands of the United States, and especially in the Ohio and Mississippi River Valleys, are the remnants of more than one hundred thousand earthen mounds that were built by humans during a span of time of more than two thousand years, from about 700 B.C.E. to about 1500 C.E. Some of the mounds are among the most colossal structures of antiquity; the base of the largest one, in southern Illinois, encompasses an area greater than that of the Great Pyramid of Egypt. Many others are built in the shape of birds or animals, and some are so large their shapes can only be fully appreciated when viewed from the air. One of these, the Great Serpent Mound, in southwestern Ohio, stretches for 1,130 feet (343 meters). Others form intricate geometrical designs. Many others are simple conical-shaped burial mounds, of varying size.

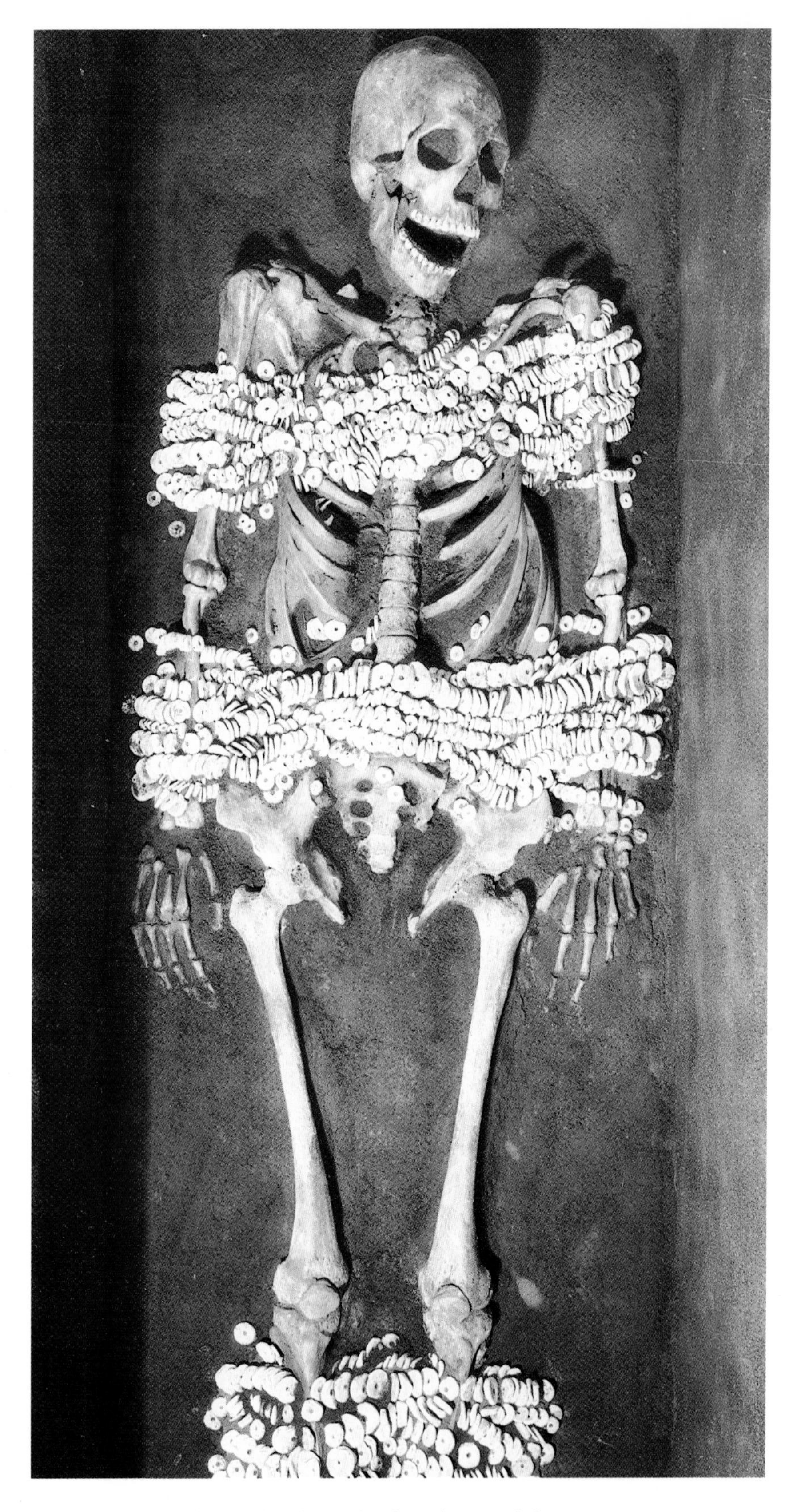

This skeleton, elaborately adorned at burial around the shoulders, waist, and legs with long strands comprising nearly two thousand shells, gives some evidence of the Mound Builder Culture's reverence for the remains of the dead.

Who built these mounds, and why, is a question that has occupied, in the view of many scholars, some of the slowest thinkers in the history of science. Until only about one hundred years ago, U.S. scientists refused to believe that the mounds could have been built by Indians. Locked into a belief in their own racial superiority, a belief made necessary by their need to justify the European conquest of the continent, Euro-Americans could not think of Indians in any terms except as primitive people incapable of creating such impressive structures. Someone else, some "vanished" civilization, had to have been the Mound Builders, so they said. Most speculation favored some European group. One study in 1787 argued that Danes had built them. A study in 1812 decided that they had been built by the Welsh. In 1820, another study concluded that they were built by the Hindus. In 1848, a study decided they might have been built by Aztecs or Mayans, but not by local Indians. Finally, in the 1880s, Congress authorized funds for the Bureau of Ethnology to look into the matter, and Cyrus Thomas was appointed to head the Division of Mound Exploration. With the publication of his report in 1894, the scientific community finally agreed that American Indians had built the mounds.

In the century since Thomas published his findings, much has been learned about the Mound Builders. We now know that there were at least three distinct mound building cultures. The oldest, called the Adena, lasted from about 700 B.C.E. until about

400 C.E. The second, called Hopewell, began about 100 B.C.E. and lasted until as late as 600 C.E., at least in some areas. The third and last culture, called Mississippian, had begun to emerge by about 800 C.E. and was in serious decline by the year 1500. But at least one example of the Mississippian Culture, the Natchez, was still thriving when the French settled in the lower Mississippi River Valley in the early eighteenth century. The Adena and Hopewell cultures built a wide variety of mounds, many of them burial mounds, but many of them also in geometrical designs and in animal shapes. The Mississippians built mounds, often very large ones, as elevated bases for large wooden structures, which were probably temples.

A reverence for the remains of the dead, such as that displayed by the Adena and Hopewell Cultures, was not a feature of Paleo-Indian culture during the Ice Age in North America. No skeletal remains from the Ice Age Clovis and Folsom Cultures, for example, have ever been found. Sometime during the last stages of the Archaic period, which followed the Ice Age, Archaic period people living in present-day Ohio entered into cultural changes that caused them to begin to revere the remains of their dead. As these people gradually evolved the Mound Builder Culture, their desire to acquire luxury items to bury with their dead had repercussions for all people living in the eastern half of the continent. These early Mound Builders had to conduct trade over great distances to acquire precious raw materials such as copper and seashells from which to fashion the luxury items, and contact between the different regions of the continent was something that had not been happening regularly for a long time.

Early Mound Builder trade constituted a revival of contact between different regions, which had become infrequent during the Archaic period. Groups of Paleo-Indians during the Ice Age had frequent contact with one another over large portions of the continent. We know this to have been the case because artifacts from that era, such as Clovis points, are found everywhere and are virtually identical, implying a widespread uniformity of culture, with frequent contact among its geographically dispersed members. During the following Archaic period, however, when the glaciers retreated and the tundra was gradually replaced by forests, and Ice Age animals disappeared, human populations became much more localized, finding adequate plant and animal food at predictable locations within their range at the same time of year, year after year. Populations tended to become isolated from one another more or less permanently, which allowed for a great deal of cultural diversity to develop, including linguistic diversity, in a relatively short time. Because regional populations became self-sufficient, and therefore independent, contact between regions lessened dramatically.

The early Mound Builders revived contacts between different regions of the continent, but it was a different kind of contact than in the distant past. Now they traded for raw materials not to use for the necessities of life, but to fashion into the luxury items that would be placed in burials. Mound Builder culture may have developed as a next step in the expression of reverence for the dead, that of creating earthen mounds to hold their remains.

— D. L. Birchfield

SEE ALSO:
Adena Culture; Archaic Period; Bureau of American Ethnology; Cahokia; Clovis Culture; Hopewell Culture; Mississippian Culture; Serpent Mound.

MOUNT GRAHAM OBSERVATORY

The Mount Graham Observatory is under construction on Mount Graham in Arizona in the Coronado National Forest, which is managed by the U.S. Forest Service. The observatory is sponsored by the Vatican, the University of Arizona, Germany's Max Planck Institute for Radio Astronomy, and Italy's Arcetri Astrophysical Observatory. The U.S. government has also provided funds.

Mount Graham is an ancient and sacred site to the San Carlos Apaches, and many Indian rights organizations have demonstrated against the observatory. But so far, the work on the observatory continues. The sponsors of the project were going to call the observatory the "Columbus Project," but because of the sensitive nature of desecrating a sacred site and the relationship between Christopher Columbus and the Indians, the sponsors decided to give the project a more general name.

influential nineteenth-century information about the Pawnees. Born in Grand Island, Nebraska, in 1862, Murie was the son of Anna, a Pawnee of the Skiri band, and James Murie, a Scot who commanded a battalion of Pawnee scouts under Major Frank North. Murie's early years were spent in Nebraska, where he lived with his mother and an uncle after his father abandoned the family, and he attended a day school at Genoa for a short time.

Relocating to Indian Territory, present-day Oklahoma, in 1874 as part of the government's removal of the Pawnees from Nebraska, Murie attended school at the tribal agency for two years and began serving as an interpreter. In 1879, he entered the Hampton Normal and Agricultural Institute in Hampton, Virginia, where he studied various academic subjects, participated in the outing or work program, and learned the printing trade. During his time there, he wrote, edited, and set type for "From the Indians," a column in the Institute publication *The Southern Workman*.

A traditional wooden flute from the Taos Pueblo in New Mexico.

Following his graduation from Hampton in 1883, Murie returned to Indian Territory and began serving as a clerk and teacher. A year later, he took Pawnee children to Haskell Institute in Lawrence, Kansas, remaining there as a disciplinarian and drillmaster for two years. Promised an appointment as a teacher at the Pawnee school by the U.S. Commissioner of Indian Affairs, Murie was denied the job by the local Indian agent.

After a stint at farming and other jobs, Murie's work in ethnography started in the 1890s when he began assisting the anthropologist Alice C. Fletcher with her studies of Pawnee culture. In 1902, Murie became a full-time assistant to George A. Dorsey, who served as curator of anthropology at the Field Museum in Chicago and was working on studies of the Arikaras, Pawnees, Wichitas, and Caddos.

Murie eventually worked as a field researcher for the Bureau of American Ethnology and collaborated with anthropologist Clark Wissler of the American Museum of Natural History and other scholars. He also produced both published and unpublished materials. At his death on November 18, 1921, Murie's publications included several volumes of mythology and *Pawnee Indian Societies*. A major work entitled *Ceremonies of the Pawnee*, now available in a reprint edition, was first published in 1981.

SEE ALSO:
Bureau of American Ethnology; Ethnography; Hampton Institute; Haskell Indian Nations University; Nebraska; Oklahoma; Pawnee.

MUSIC AND MUSICAL INSTRUMENTS

Traditionally, American Indian music has roots deep in the relationship between the sounds of nature and people's desire to communicate the emotions of the heart. Many Native musicians and singers believe that songs often come directly from the hearts of the people through visions, and because these visions contain sacred tribal knowl-

A Navajo pottery drum, on display at the Navajo Tribal Museum in Window Rock, Arizona. Percussion instruments have long played a key role in the music of a wide variety of Native societies.

edge, the songs may also be sacred. Traditionally, Indian music developed from the strength of rushing rivers and thundering herds of buffalo, the cries of the coyote, echoes of the fish, and the songs of birds. From this point of view, music is thus a sacred bond to the natural world, like a bridge connecting the beginning of time to the present and connecting Native people today to their ancestors and other supernatural forces of the earth.

Indian music also is linked to Indian oral traditions and histories. Many of the instruments, as well as much of the music, have survived persecution and death. Songs and dances thus help the people to remember and associate important events with the whole body, not just the mind.

The sense of aesthetics, or what is beautiful and artistically valid, is very different between Western concepts and Indian concepts and ways of life. Unlike Western cultures, some tribal cultures do not have language that refers to the arts as a separate entity apart from other things in life. It is therefore important to realize that not all tribal cultures view art and music according to Western cultural or artistic standards. For example, most Indian musicians follow concepts such as these: (1) Music is inextricably linked to an action or behavior, as is dance; (2) Music is functional and is part of the everyday life of Native people; (3) Because of its spiritual and natural connections, traditional music for listening pleasure does not exist; (4) There is primarily only local music—that is, music that derives from and speaks to the local community; and (5) The idea of a composer as in Western culture does not exist.

Traditional musical instruments consisted mostly of percussion, with some wind instruments; there were no strings, unless someone played on the hunter's bow. Flutes and whistles were made of wood, clay, seashells, metal, cane poles, bird bones, reeds, and animal horns, while other instruments consisted of rattles, pebbles, and bull-roarers (a small wooden slat on a string that makes a roaring noise

Nora Naranjo-Morse, a poet and potter from Santa Clara Pueblo, New Mexico, smiles down at one of her pottery figurines.

sculpture pieces. As the title of her book *Mud Woman* suggests, in Naranjo-Morse's worldview, it is the clay that forms the potter. This way of portraying the artist's role demonstrates the Native American belief in the landscape having a part in a person's idea of herself or himself. The red clay, the central image of Naranjo-Morse's poetry, is the color of the material that she herself gathers, the color of her landscape, the color of her people, the color of her art, and the color of her heart.

Naranjo-Morse acknowledges the inspiration of Nan Chu Kweejo, Clay Mother, a kind of potter's muse or inspirational figure, thanking her for her gifts. Naranjo-Morse's uncluttered lines contain simple images delivered in a conversational storytelling style that bring to mind the feeling of an over-the-counter kitchen conversation. There is much going on below the surface of the lines, however, which are joyous.

Equally joyous are the pictures of her clay sculptures that take the poems' stories off into new and surprising directions. For instance, the poem "Mud Woman's First Encounter with the World of Money and Business" deals with an elder Santa Clara potter who takes her work to a gallery to sell. In the picture of the sculpture accompanying the poem, Mud Woman is shirtless and holding a clay piece in each hand at breast level. The photo suggests that for Mud Woman, her life work is part of her flesh and that, further, these gifts that she shapes with her own two hands are capable of nurturing, just as a woman nurtures with her body and spirit. In the poem, however, Mud Woman is exposed to the white world of art as merchandise—a world in which art is not connected with community, relatives, and ancestral voices but is judged, rather, in monetary terms.

Mud Woman, which is Naranjo-Morse's first book, contains a strong storytelling voice, lively characters, and a feeling of being rooted in her community. The pictures of Naranjo-Morse's sculptures also have a narrative, or storytelling, quality; they complement and expand the storytelling of the poems. As shown in the figure of Mud Woman and in the poems about her, words and clay work together to form characters, and Naranjo-Morse arranges pieces of poetry and sculpture together in repose and in conversation, causing them to come alive.

A close-up of a pottery figurine titled *Uncle Fidel's Cousin San Luis* by artist Nora Naranjo-Morse.

In this photo, taken in 1926, a man identified by his lapel button as "Chief Sunset, Full Blooded Narragansett Indian," wears an assortment of decorative attire, including an American flag, stitched onto his coat.

One of Naranjo-Morse's characters, Pearlene, is especially interesting. Pearlene is a woman who sets her own limits and makes her own choices, ignoring the community gossip about her. Pearlene stands outside the cultural standards of her community, and the poems raise the question of whether the tension this causes between an individual and her community might actually be healthy, that a woman like Pearlene might be a kind of "glue" to her community that increases the community's ties to one another rather than destroying them.

Pearlene is the one brave enough to actually do the things the rest of the community only fantasizes about. Pearlene's behavior, which involves an acceptance of modern lifestyles and sexual freedom, is troubling to her community, but in spite of her behavior, a legacy remains of her Pueblo heritage. She has had "too many men / and long nights / at nameless bars," yet "She was a Towa, / beneath that veneer / of Avon / and fast, / hard times."

Pearlene's life demonstrates both the problems and the creative possibilities of merging past and present, and she raises the issue of how one creatively gets in touch with his or her own roots. The poems suggest that perhaps Pearlene achieves this balance in spite of her unapproved behavior.

See also:
Kiva; Pueblo.

NARRAGANSETT

At their height during the seventeeth century in the region that came to be called New England, the Narragansetts, with Canonicus as their most influential leader, held sway over the area from Narragansett Bay on the east to the Pawcatuck River on the west. The Narragansetts were rarely warlike, but their large numbers (about four thousand men of warrior age in the early seventeenth century) usually prevented other Native nations from attacking them.

William Wood, in *New England's Prospect*, characterized the Narragansetts as "the most numerous people in those parts, and the most rich also, and the most industrious, being a storehouse of all kinds . . . of merchandise. . . ." The Narragansetts fashioned wampum in bracelets and pendants for many other Indians. They also made smoking pipes "much desired by our English tobacconists for their rarity, strength, handsomeness, and coolness."

According to Wood's account, the Narragansetts had never desired "to take part in any martial enterprise. But being incapable of a jeer, they rest secure under the conceit of their popularity, and seek rather to grow rich by industry than famous by deeds of chivalry." In this fashion, the Narragansetts built a confederacy in which they supervised the affairs of Indian peoples throughout most of present-day Rhode Island and eastern Long Island, New York, about thirty thousand Native people in the early seventeenth century.

Canonicus was a close friend of Roger Williams, the Puritan dissident who founded Providence Plantations, which was later named Rhode Island. Very quickly, Williams's house in Narragansett Country became a transcultural meeting place. He lodged as many as fifty Indians at a time—travelers, traders, and sachems on their way to or from treaty conferences. If a Puritan needed to contact an Indian, or vice versa, he more than likely did so with Williams's aid. Among Indian nations at odds with each other, Williams became "a quencher of our fires."

When word reached Boston that the Pequots were rallying other Indian nations to drive the Massachusetts Bay settlements into the sea, the Massachusetts Council sent urgent pleas to Williams to use his "utmost and speediest Endeavors" to keep the Narragansetts out of it. Within hours after the appeal arrived in the hands of an Indian runner, "scarce acquainting my wife," Williams boarded "a poor Canow & . . . cut through a stormie Wind and with great seas, euery [*sic*] minute in hazard of life to the Sachim's [Canonicus's] howse." After traveling thirty miles (forty-eight kilometers) in the storm, Williams put into port in a Narragansett town larger than most of the English settlements of his day, knowing that the success or failure of the Pequot initiative might rest on whether he could dissuade his friends from joining them in the uprising.

Canonicus listened to Williams with Mixanno at his side. The younger sachem was assuming the duties of leadership piecemeal as his father aged. The three men decided to seal an alliance, and within a few days, officials from Boston were hurrying through the forest to complete the necessary paperwork. The Puritan deputies were awed at the size of the Narragansett town, as well as the size of the hall in which they negotiated the alliance. The structure, about fifty feet (fifteen meters) wide, was likened to a statehouse by the men from Boston.

The outcome of the Pequot War during the summer of 1636, in which the balance of power shifted away from the Pequots and their allies and toward the colonists and their Native alliance, radically altered the demographic balance in New England. Before it, the English colonists were a tiny minority. After it, they were unquestionably dominant.

SEE ALSO:
Canonicus; King Philip's War; Massachusetts; Massasoit; Pequot War; Rhode Island; Wampanoag; Wampum.

NASNAGA (1941–)

Nasnaga is the Indian name of author Roger Russell. He was born in 1941 and he is a member of the Shawnee tribe. As well as being a writer, Nasnaga is also an artist and a draftsman.

Nasnaga is the author of one novel, *Indians' Summer*, published in 1975. In the novel, the Navajo, Mohawk, Apache, and Pueblo Nations declare their independence from the United States on July 4, 1976, upsetting plans for bicentennial festivities. The Indians seize National Guard equipment and munitions and seal off large parts of New Mexico, Oklahoma, and South Dakota, and they close the U.S.–Canadian border at Quebec and New York. The Indians also occupy Minuteman nuclear missile sites and threaten to blow up Washington, D.C., if their request for independence is not met. In their fight, the Indians gain help and recognition from India and other developing nations.

NATIONAL CONGRESS OF AMERICAN INDIANS

SEE Activism, Indian.

NATIONAL INDIAN GAMING COMMISSION

The National Indian Gaming Commission was formed through the passage of the Indian Gaming Regulatory Act of 1988. The act was created to strengthen the Bureau of Indian Affairs' responsibility in the operation of Indian gaming facilities as tribal governments were finding a new economic independence in casinos and high-stakes gambling operations.

The act established the commission within the Department of the Interior to create rules and regulations concerning Indian gaming operations. Working with the various tribes that have gaming operations, the commission regulates Class II gaming, which includes bingo and similar games. Critics of the commission and of the act that created it point out that the commission is one more example of the U.S. government's reluctance to accept the sovereign right of Indian tribes to financial independence—particularly in the face of the newly found freedom that operating gaming facilities first offered the tribes.

Despite these criticisms, however, Native gaming organizations made up of volunteers from various tribal governments do have a voice within the commission. Many tribal representatives are now concerned that, as more and more tribes enter into the gaming field and the quick cure that gaming seemed to offer poverty-torn reservations is spread out over many more tribes, the quick boost in tribal economies will level off and may cease entirely.

SEE ALSO:
Bureau of Indian Affairs; Gaming; Indian Gaming Regulatory Act of 1988; Self-determination; Tribal Sovereignty.

NATIONS, INDIAN

As a political term, *nation* refers to a government that is independent from any other government, possessing the power of absolute dominion over its territory and people. The terms *nation*, *tribe*, or *band* are used interchangeably in many Indian

A highway sign advertising an Indian high-stakes bingo casino in California. U.S. government controls over gaming as a source of tribal revenue are an example of the restrictions placed by Congress on Indian nations' right to self-governance.

treaties and statutes. The idea of Indian tribes being nations and having the inherent right of tribal sovereignty was first acknowledged by the United States Supreme Court in 1832 in the case of *Worcester v. Georgia.* The Court found that Georgia could not extend its laws within the Cherokee Nation.

Prior to the *Worcester* decision, treaties with Indian tribes were deemed equal to U.S. treaties with foreign nations in validity and effect. Federal courts repeatedly agreed. In 1828, Attorney General William Wirt provided a legal opinion to the president about the issue presented by the state of Georgia questioning the effect of Indian treaties. Georgia argued that Indian treaties were not effective because they were not treaties with an independent nation, and even if independent, the Indians were "uncivilized." The attorney general concluded that they are "as free, sovereign, and independent as any other nation. . . . Nor can it be conceded that their [the Indians'] independence as a nation is a limited independence. Like all other independent nations, they are governed solely by their own laws. Like all other independent nations, they have the absolute power of war and peace. Like all other independent nations, their territory is inviolable by any other sovereignty. . . . As a nation they are still free and independent. They are entirely self-governed—self-directed. They treat, or refuse to treat, at their pleasure; and there is no human power which can rightfully control them in the exercise of their discretion in this respect. In their treaties, in all their contracts with regard to their property, they are as free, sovereign, and independent as any other nation."

Today, Indian governments are not independent because their governmental authority has been taken from them—many claim without legal justification—by the United States Congress. Congress claims that it can limit or completely abolish the tribal government if it chooses to do so. However, *until* Congress limits or abolishes the tribes' right of self-government, the tribes retain their existing sovereign powers.

The Indian Civil Rights Act (ICRA) of 1968 and the Indian Gaming Regulatory Act (IGRA) of 1988 are examples of limits placed by Congress on a tribe's inherent power to regulate internal matters. These acts restrict tribal sovereignty. Although the ICRA provides to tribal members the basic freedoms and due process protections guaranteed to United States citizens by the United States Constitution, it also places certain restrictions on a tribe's ability to arrest and prosecute criminal offenders. The IGRA restricts gaming activities on Indian lands, establishing (1) independent federal regulatory authority, (2) federal standards, and (3) the National Indian Gaming Commission. However, it also shields the tribe from organized crime and other corrupting influences, ensures that the tribe is the primary beneficiary of the gaming operation, and assures the public that gaming is conducted fairly and honestly by both the operator and the players.

The ICRA and the IGRA are but two instances of specific limits placed by Congress on a tribe's right to self-governance. How many sovereign powers and which powers—and how much right of tribal self-government—are left to the various nations has been a topic debated and subjected to numerous hearings, laws, and legal decisions since the beginning of Indian America's formal dealings with the United States and various state governments.

SEE ALSO:
American Indian Civil Rights Act of 1968; Indian Gaming Regulatory Act of 1988; Indian Major Crimes Act; National Indian Gaming Commission; Self-determination; Self-determination Policy; Tribal Sovereignty; *Worcester v. Georgia.*

NATIVE AMERICAN

Native American is a relatively new term and is used to refer to the original inhabitants of the United States. It did not appear in any dictionary until 1959, when it made its debut in a Scribner's dictionary. But dictionaries do not create words; they merely reflect usage. Therefore, the term Native American had to have been in use long enough for it to come to the attention of lexicographers before it could be added to a dictionary.

Indigenous peoples of Canada have historically been referred to as *aborigines* by white Canadians, but indigenous peoples of that area now frequently refer to themselves as *First Nations People.* South American Indians are not always known as Native

Americans. Also, Native people from Alaska are generally not referred to in federal legislation as Native Americans but are referred to as *Alaskan Natives*.

The term *Indian* is a historical oddity. Columbus thought that he had reached the country of India when he arrived in the Caribbean. The Spanish created a Council of the Indies to govern the area, and the term *Indian* derived from that usage and was later adopted by other Europeans. *Indian* has been widely used in historical writings and in federal treaties and statutes and by Native people themselves. Native people in the United States are accustomed to its usage and frequently use the term in the name of organizations that they create for themselves. They also frequently use the term *Native American*. And although some Native people feel that the term *Indian* distinguishes them from non-Natives who also claim to be "native" to the United States, there doesn't seem to be a preference among Native people between the two terms.

SEE ALSO:
American Indians; India.

NATIVE AMERICAN AWARENESS

A presidential executive order declares November each year as Indian Heritage Month to honor the contributions of Native Americans. During that month, many federal agencies sponsor programs featuring Native arts and crafts, food, and ceremonial songs and dances. The programs also provide Indian speakers to educate the public about Indian culture, lifestyles, and ideas. These speakers address stereotypical ideas held by many non-Indians—for example, that Indians once said "How" as a greeting, introduced scalping in battle, are a savage and hostile people, currently live in tipis and wear regalia for everyday use, or are perpetually drunk. In addition to debunking these negative images, these speakers also explain positive contributions made by Indians to North American society.

The Boy Scouts of America have a long history of respectful appreciation for Indian culture. At their jamborees, which are often called powwows, it is customary for Boy Scouts to don the regalia of Native Americans and do dances based on Native traditions. Today, Indian powwows are widespread and popularly attended by many non-Indians, who can experience Native dances, crafts, and food.

The American Indian Movement (AIM) has also been instrumental in educating the public to the plight of Indians. The civil rights movement also affected the civil rights of Indians, resulting in congressional passage of the Indian Civil Rights Act.

Notable actors and actresses, such as Marlon Brando and Jane Fonda, showed open support for Native Americans at various points in their careers, making Indians and their culture not only acceptable, but perhaps even chic. Movie producers of the 1990s have featured Indians actually playing the role of the key Indian characters, unlike earlier movies in which Indians have often been portrayed by non-Indian actors. The movie *Dances with Wolves* is a good example, featuring Indian actors and showing more accuracy in the depiction of Indians and portraying more human and less stereotypical characteristics and behavior. The movie's box-office success demonstrated that portraying Indians more realistically was acceptable to members of a society whose early popular images of Indian people had been shaped by stereotype and the oversimplification of relations between early Euro-Americans and Natives.

Despite these gains in awareness of Native cultures, history, and traditions among mainstream Americans, many critics point out that there may also be a tendency among non-Natives to go too far in their efforts. Much of the interest in Indian lifestyles has led to another form of oversimplification and stereotyping, which although it may portray Indian people more favorably, may still be inaccurate and disrespectful of Native attitudes and spirituality. In this respect, non-Natives who embellish their understanding of Indian life with fanciful and romantic images of "primitive" or "noble" Native people may be blinding themselves to the harsher and less pleasant realities of life on reservations or in the cities for many Indian people.

SEE ALSO:
American Indian Movement; European Attitudes Toward Indigenous Peoples; Hollywood, Indians, and Indian Images; Native American Contributions; New Age Movement; Scalping; Tomahawk Chop.

NATIVE AMERICAN CHURCH

One of the most effective responses to the severe repression of Native peoples and cultures at the turn of the century was religious. After the Ghost Dance played a role in the massacre at Wounded Knee, most practices of Native religions went underground. The Native American Church is historically important not only because it preserved Native culture underground (and thus kept alive forms of community that were being lost to assimilation), but also because it was an early example of a successful pan-Indian movement.

Like the Longhouse religion begun by the Iroquois Handsome Lake a century earlier, the Native American Church sought Indian members only and sometimes carried the air of a secret society, especially in the eyes of non-Indians. Both religions rejected aspects of European culture that had proved especially harmful to Native American people, particularly alcohol; both religions mixed Native belief and custom with some aspects of Christianity. Both continue to attract adherents today.

The secrecy of the Native American Church, at least to non-Indian eyes, caused some of these

A Navajo Native American Church hogan in Aneth, Utah, displays symbols that combine Native, Christian, and patriotic U.S. themes. The Native American Church has long held appeal for Indian people of varying religious and spiritual backgrounds.

observers to cry "paganism." The practice that brought down the wrath of European-Americans on the church's members was their use of peyote. Chewing the peyote bean produces mild hallucinations; in the early years of the Native American Church, members took peyote to aid meditation, as a religious sacrament, and to blunt the pain and alienation of reservation life.

The so-called peyote cult arose in Mexico and spread among the Apaches and Comanches during the 1870s. After the decline of the Ghost Dance Religion in the 1890s, the use of peyote in religious ceremonies swept over the Plains in the central part of North America. The Native American Church itself was founded in 1918. By 1955, people belonging to roughly eighty Native tribes and nations practiced some form of ceremonial use.

Some of the opposition to this use of peyote came from nonpracticing Native Americans. In 1940, the Navajo Tribal Council, dominated by Christians, outlawed its use. The Taos Pueblos, White Mountain Apaches, and several Sioux communities passed laws forbidding the use of peyote. Many of these were enacted in response to the urgent requests of traditionalists, who saw the Native American Church as a threat to existing tribal religions. The territorial legislature of Oklahoma outlawed its use in 1898, and by 1923, fourteen states had banned the use of peyote. Customs agents began seizing peyote crossing the U.S. border with Mexico. In 1940, Congress outlawed the shipment of peyote through the mail. The Bureau of Indian Affairs tried to enact laws to ban the use of peyote nationwide, but this effort failed since not enough non-Indians used peyote to fuel a drug scare.

Compared to many Native religions, the Native American Church is a relatively recent development. However, it is one that fits the needs of many modern Native Americans. It stresses leading a moral life and the moral unity of all Indian peoples, integrating religious symbols from many nations. The Native American Church continues to fight for religious freedom.

See also:
Ghost Dance Religion; Handsome Lake; Longhouse Religion; Wounded Knee (1890).

NATIVE AMERICAN CONTRIBUTIONS

The idea that Native American peoples "contributed" to North, South, and Central American societies may seem a bit perplexing, considering that prior to contact with European explorers, missionaries, settlers, and conquerors, the Americas comprised only Native cultures. And yet, following European contact, many of the foods, agricultural products, medicines, technologies, and political philosophies of Native America began to be known to other parts of the world. Thus, we may speak of Native American contributions not only to the American cultures, but also to societies in Europe, Asia, and Africa.

Food

Probably one of the most important contributions by Native peoples to American culture has been food. It is estimated that 70 to 75 percent of foods and food products used today had their beginnings in Native American gardens, fields, forests, hillsides, mountains, lakes, rivers, and oceans. In contrast to the unfavorable descriptions of early Native peoples in European-oriented historical accounts, the Indians actually lived and ate well. This is primarily because they had considerable skill in horticulture, agriculture, food processing and development, and wildlife management.

To take just a few examples, the potato, or *papa*, as the Quechuas call it, is believed to have been cultivated in the Andes for over four thousand years. The Incas developed 3,000 varieties of the potato, of which the United States currently uses only 250. Of those, only 20 varieties make up 75 percent of the total U.S. potato crop. At the local market, shoppers are likely to find only a handful of the possible varieties, such as russet, white, yellow fin, white fin, red, and Yukon. Other varieties are just now being cultivated widely after five hundred years. The reason the potato is so important is that it has almost twice the nutritional value of most European grains, it grows in half the time with much less care, and it grows in a variety of conditions and soils. An added attraction is that the potato does not have to be milled or processed to become edible.

Beans are another food grown and eaten for centuries by Native peoples. The Narragansetts of

Baking bread in a traditional oven at Taos Pueblo, New Mexico.

New England, for example, put together a mixture of lima beans, peppers, and corn, making a dish called succotash. Beans have been cultivated in a number of varieties and are found under a large variety of names. Some of these names—such as the Madagascar bean and Rangoon bean—might suggest that the beans come from those places. In fact, many of the foods called beans originated in the Americas, particularly Central America, although many varieties were used in North and South America as well. Beans today are highly rated by nutritionists and diners alike for their protein and nutritional value, as well as for their many flavors. Beans in common use today include black, butter, Burma, common Indian red, French, kidney, lima, Madagascar, navy, pinto, pole, Rangoon, snap, string, tepary, and white. There are other varieties that have not yet found their way to North American tables.

Probably the best-known food contribution of Native Americans to the rest of the world is corn. Historians have recently determined that corn has been cultivated in the Americas for somewhere between five thousand and seven thousand years. As with most American breeds, there are many varieties: sweet, dent, popcorn, flint, yellow, white, and what is called Indian corn, which comes in a variety of colors. Within these varieties are crossbreeds as well. In ancient times, Native peoples used corn for a large variety of foods, including cornmeal (or corn flour), enchiladas, fry bread, grits (or hominy), piki bread, corn fritters, corn bread, corn chowder, polenta (or cornmeal mush), tamale wrappers, and tortillas (flat bread). More recent uses include corn butter, corn liquor, corn oil, cornstarch, corn syrup, and livestock feed. Some very contemporary products include corn dogs, nachos, tortilla chips, taco shells, corn chips, and Cracker Jacks (popped corn covered with maple syrup).

Chiles, which are native to Central America, are another well-known and internationally well-loved food. Many Asian countries have developed a special love for chiles. Southern China, India,

Sri Lanka, and Thailand, for example, have made the chile their own, so much so that many believe the chile originated in those places. There are about seventy-five varieties of chiles. The most common are fresh chiles, which include Anaheim, ancho, cayenne, Cubanelle, Fresno, güero, habanero, jalapeño, New Mexico green, New Mexico red, pepperoncini, pimento, poblano, serrano, and Thai. Dried chiles include ancho, California, cascabel, Chinese red, chipotle, de arbol, guajillo, japones, mulato, New Mexico green, New Mexico red, pasilla, and pequin. Powdered chiles include ancho, Caribe, California, cayenne pepper, chimayo, molido, and paprika.

Grains are usually not associated with the Americas because it is believed that Native peoples did not use many grains other than corn. Two indigenous grains, however, are just now making it to American markets: *amaranth* and *quinoa*. Amaranth (*kiwicha*) was a mainstay of the Aztec diet. It is rich in lysine, an amino acid that is not found in other grains, and it contains more protein than any other grain except for quinoa. Amaranth is used extensively in other countries, including India, Pakistan, Tibet, Nepal, and China. Quinoa, cultivated by the Incas, has eight amino acids that the body cannot produce. The seed itself has a bad-tasting natural resin coat that protects it from pests. This coating must be washed off before cooking.

The tomato is another well-traveled product of the Americas. Italians use tomatoes extensively and have bred some of their own from the original stock. All tomatoes originated in the Americas. Some common types include yellow, orange, green, and red. Sizes run from golf-ball size to almost melon size. Throughout the world, tomatoes are used in salads, chili, pizza, ketchup, spaghetti, ravioli, lasagna, meat sauces, salsa, and many other dishes.

Squashes, or, as the Narragansetts called them, *askootasquash*, are not as widely known as some other Native food products, but they have a large following in the Americas. Italian-Americans have

Mesquite bean pods at a display of Native contributions to North American culture in California.

A group of Miwok Indians prepare bison meat over an outdoor fire—what most North Americans call a barbecue—at a gathering at Indian Grinding Rock State Park in Volcano, California.

enthusiastically adopted the zucchini, for example. The pumpkin has become a symbol associated with both Halloween and Thanksgiving. Squashes are rich in carotene, which is transformed into vitamin A in the liver. Squashes are also recommended for the prevention of certain types of cancer.

Berries that were a part of the Native diet include bearberry, blackberry, blueberry (twenty varieties!), buffaloberry, ground cherry, chokecherry, cloudberry, cranberry, wild currants, elderberry, gooseberry, wild grapes, hackberry, huckleberry, juneberry, manzanita, raspberry, salalberry, sarsaparilla, saskatoon, snowberry, soapberry, and berries of juniper, Solomon's seal, spicebush, and sumac. The Indians also made use of tree products, including allspice, chewing gum, and maple syrup.

Native peoples enjoyed a variety of fruits, including avocados, cacao (chocolate), guava, maracuya, papaya, passion fruit, maypop, persimmon, pineapple, squash blossoms, tomatillos, vanilla, and wild plum. The types of nuts they ate included acorn, beechnut, black walnut, Brazil, butternut, cashew, chestnut, chinkapin, hazelnut, hickory nut, peanut, pecan, and pine nut. Native peoples also made use of roots in their diet, including cassava root (today cassava can be found in tapioca and meat tenderizer), ginseng root, prairie turnips, sassafras root (the main ingredient in root beer), and sweet potato.

Native Americans incorporated a number of meats and seafoods in their diets as well. These included abalone, alligator, antelope, armadillo, bluefish, buffalo (or bison), catfish, clam, crab, crawfish, elk, frog, guinea pig, halibut, lobster, muskrat, mussels, prairie chicken, tuna, quail, rabbit, rattlesnake, whale (gray and humpback, for example), salmon, seal, seaweed, shrimp, turtle (including green and snapping), sturgeon, trout, turkey (both wild and domesticated), and white-tailed deer.

Some Native foods were adopted by European immigrants but given different names. For exam-

A mule's ear plant. Native societies have used the seeds from this plant for making flour, and the plant's root, which is slightly bitter and aromatic, has been used to treat throat disorders.

ple, Native American people had a variety of soft drinks, or native tonics, made from spices and fruits. Many were consumed as medicines. Some, such as root beer and coca drinks, made the transition to the European-American diet but lost some of their ingredients. Later, carbonation was added and they became "pop." Other products not so appealing to the Europeans but still a part of some American Indian diets include Indian celery shoots, herring eggs right out of the water, octopus, many varieties of dried seaweed, pemmican (dried mixed venison and berries), fiddlehead fern tops, whale blubber (especially rich in vitamin C), dried halibut in seal oil, fish heads, sea urchin, and salmon eggs, to mention only a few.

Medicine

Much of the world's current pharmacology—an estimated 70 percent—also has Native American origins. By the time Europeans began emigrating to the Americas, there were few herbalists and medicine people left in Europe. Most had been executed in the Dark Ages, having been accused of heresy and consorting with the devil. As it was, much of Native American medicine was eliminated by the Catholic Church early in the days of European colonization, particularly in Central America. The north, however, was settled less forcibly. This helped preserve much of the old knowledge, even though the Native Americans were never really given credit for it.

For example, the treatment for scurvy was "discovered" by James Lind, a Scottish naval doctor, some 260 years after the cure was stumbled upon by the early French explorer Jacques Cartier. In 1535, while stranded on the St. Lawrence River by ice, Cartier's crew of 110 men took on the symptoms of scurvy, and 25 of them subsequently died. Cartier noticed that the local Hurons had shown the early symptoms of the disease but soon recovered. After some of his crew died, Cartier finally got up the courage and asked the Natives about their cure. The local Huron chief shared their "miracle cure"—vitamin C—and the rest of Cartier's crew recovered. The Hurons obtained their vitamin C by making pine needle and bark tonics from a type of evergreen tree in the region. He entered the whole incident in his log, which Lind read many years later. Lind took credit for the "discovery," and eventually British naval ships were required to carry limes on board to avoid scurvy. This European method of "discovery," unfortunately, would continue on through the years, and the Indians would rarely get credit for their contributions.

Other medicines and medical treatments used by Native Americans include alumroot and witch hazel, as well as leaves and bark extracts as astringents, detergents, purgatives, and laxatives. To heal flesh wounds, Native peoples used different types of balms, such as balsam fir, elder flowers, and oil of wintergreen. Common ointments and oils included aloe vera for general burns and skin rashes, jojoba oil, and petroleum jelly. They made cough syrup from a variety of natural substances, including wild cherry bark and licorice root. Curare was used as a muscle relaxant. Vermifuge was used as an emetic to induce vomiting, ipecac as a cure for amoebic dysentery, pink root as a narcotic, and dogwood to reduce fever.

Hallucinogens used by Native Americans included the Doña Ana cactus, mescal beans, peyote cactus, and psilocybin mushrooms, called *teonanacatl*. For laxatives, Native peoples used buckthorn, called "sacred bark" by the Spanish, which is also a diuretic.

Medicinal herbal teas were brewed from annedda needles (high in vitamin C), coca, ginseng, juniper berries, sage, and sassafras. Pau d'arco (*taheebo*) was used to treat inflammatory diseases as well as cancers and tumors. Candida was used to treat yeast infections, as were tobacco and mint marigold.

Painkillers included willow and coca, which also prevents altitude sickness. Preventative med-

An undated photo of a sweat lodge in a Crow village in Montana. The use of sweat baths and steam rooms holds an appeal not only to Natives but to other North Americans seeking both physical and spiritual purification.

A dugout canoe in the works on the Hoh Reservation on the Olympic Peninsula, Washington State. The art, craft, and technology of building canoes and other boats has long been an area of expertise in various Native cultures.

icines included kelp, which is high in iodine and thus prevents and cures goiter; quinine, which treats malaria; and the use of sweat baths. Stimulants included boneset and sage.

Technology

Spiritual, intellectual, and physical balance is central to Native American culture. This respectful and holistic approach to the environment was largely ignored by Europeans because it often got in the way of profit. Nonetheless, a number of technological contributions by Native Americans have been recognized and used in the early years of the United States.

There were many canoe technologies throughout the Americas. Many people are familiar with the birch bark canoe and the dugout of the Pacific Northwest, but the kayak is an Inuit contribution. These days, it is used mostly for recreation, but for the Inuits it was invaluable. A good craft could not only keep a village in food but could save a life as well, because it righted if capsized by a whale or walrus. Women made these vessels of wood, bone, and seal skin, fashioning them like an item of clothing. In fact, a man did not so much ride in a kayak as put it on.

Another Native contribution to transportation was the snowshoe. When they first arrived in the Americas, the Europeans had great difficulty traveling around, especially in the north when there was snow on the ground. They tried to ski but found this limiting because of the roughness of the terrain and the difficulty of carrying a load while on skis. Centuries earlier, the Natives had solved this problem with the invention of the snowshoe. Made of spruce and rawhide, it was light and could carry substantial weight. For additional loads, they used dogs, and for even heavier loads, toboggans and the cariole sleds.

Agricultural development was another area in which Native peoples excelled. The early European explorers, for example, were amazed to find fine cotton garments in use by the Indians. The Europeans had a coarse type of cotton used mostly

Hauling a birchwood sled, a Cree man sets out on snowshoes for a day of trapping in subarctic Quebec. It takes a certain amount of skill and patience, but using snowshoes has become both a practical means of transportation and a popular form of winter recreation.

as batting, padding, and stuffing, but the quality of the Indian cotton was so fine, the Europeans initially thought it was silk. The new cotton had a longer strand, and the Incas had developed the processing and weaving technology to go along with it. It became a major industry.

In addition, dyes that the Indians made from a Brazilian tree (for purple) and the scales of the female insect *Dactylopius coccus* (for red) were items of commerce coveted by the Europeans. This dye, called cochineal dye, was used in the famous red uniforms of British soldiers, who were known as redcoats. One pound (0.45 kilogram) of dye required the processing of up to seventy thousand insects. A yellow made from annatto tree seed was used for food coloring and as a fine fabric dye. In addition, there were Native techniques for reproducing certain plants from cuttings, either when a hybrid plant could no longer reproduce itself or when seeds could not be obtained.

Along with all the food that came from the Americas, Native Americans also made contributions in food-processing technology. Although most foods were fairly simple—they simply required picking and cooking—others were more complex, such as corn syrup and maple syrup, which required an extra step to process. Another example is Pika bread, where the corn flour has to be soaked in lime made from wood ash. This process adds calcium and niacin, which makes the bread even more nutritious.

In the area of forest management, one of the things that amazed Europeans was the parklike quality of the American forests. It was easy to move around, collect forest products, and hunt game. They thought that this was the natural state of things. But it was no accident that these forests were so clear. For many years, the Native peoples maintained certain areas just for the purpose of growing food and hunting. This was done by burning and clearing the underbrush, thinning out trees, and managing crops.

So-called slash-and-burn clearing is a means of opening up land for growing crops in forested

cational institutions and organizations. The organization is funded by the Corporation for Public Broadcasting, its public television and public radio members, and the Nebraska Educational TV Network. The organization also receives private funding for its work with Native American productions.

SEE ALSO:
Native American Journalists Association.

FOR FURTHER INFORMATION ABOUT NAPBC:
Native American Public
Broadcasting Consortium
P. O. Box 83111
1800 North 33rd Street
Lincoln, NE 68501–3111
402-472-3522
Fax 402-472-1785

NAVAJO

In 1987, approximately 125,000 Navajos living on the Navajo Nation still spoke Navajo fluently. Navajo is an Athabascan language. The Athabascan language family has four branches—Northern Athabascan, Southwestern Athabascan, Pacific Coast Athabascan, and Eyak, from southeast Alaska. The Athabascan language family is one of three families within the Na-Dene language division; the other two, the Tlingit family and the Haida family, are isolated languages in the far north—Tlingit in southeast Alaska and Haida in British Columbia. Na-Dene is one of the most widely distributed language divisions in North America. The Southwestern Athabascan language, sometimes called Apachean, has seven dialects: Navajo, Western Apache, Chiricahua, Mescalero, Jicarilla, Lipan, and Kiowa-Apache.

KSUT, a Ute radio station in Ignacio, Colorado, is one of many Native public stations that are eligible to benefit from the archives and technical support offered by the Native American Public Broadcasting Consortium.

Shirlene Begay, a Navajo second-grader at the Rock Point Community School, Arizona, holds a self-portrait with text written in her local tongue.

It is not known, and will probably never be known, exactly when the Navajos and Apaches (the Southwestern Athabascans) began migrating from the far north to the Southwest or what route they took. Linguists who study changes in language and then estimate how long related languages have been separated have offered the year 1000 C.E. as an approximate date for the migration's beginning. But it is clear that the Southwestern Athabascans did not arrive in the Southwest until at least the end of the fourteenth century.

Until that time, what is now known as the Navajo homeland was inhabited by one of the most remarkable civilizations of ancient people in North America, the Anasazi. Anasazi ruins are among the most spectacular in North America, especially their elaborate cliff dwellings, such as the ones at Mesa Verde National Park, but also including such communities as Chaco Canyon, where multistory stone masonry apartment buildings and large underground kivas (ceremonial chambers) can still be seen today. Scholars originally thought that the arrival of the Southern Athabascans in the Southwest was a factor in the collapse of the Anasazi civilization, but it is now known that the Anasazi agricultural culture could not withstand the severe prolonged droughts that occurred at the end of the fourteenth century. In all likelihood, the Anasazi had moved to the more dependable sources of water along the watershed of the upper Rio Grande and had reestablished themselves as the Pueblo peoples by the time the Navajos entered the Southwest.

The Navajos then claimed this empty land as their own. They first settled in what they call Dinetah ("among the Navajo"), in the far northwestern corner of New Mexico. After they had acquired sheep and horses from the Spanish, which revolutionized their lives, and acquired cultural and material attributes from the Pueblos, which further enhanced their ability to adjust to the environment of the Southwest, the Navajos then spread out into all of Dine Bikeyah, "the Navajo Country."

Navajos lived too far from the Spanish in New Mexico, who were concentrated in the upper Rio

Seen from the air, Navajo farms seem dwarfed by the spectacular landscape of Canyon de Chelly, Arizona.

A Navajo family poses outside of their hogan in the portion of the Navajo Nation located in Arizona.

Grande Valley, to be subjected to the disruption of their lives that the Pueblos suffered at the hands of the Spanish. At times, the Navajos were allied with the Spanish against other Indians, principally the Utes, and at times, the Spanish allied with the Utes and fought the Navajos. For the Navajos, the most important by-product of the Spanish colonies in New Mexico was the introduction of horses and sheep (the smooth, nonoily wool of the Spanish sheep would prove ideal for weaving).

When the United States claimed that it had acquired an interest in Navajo land by virtue of having won a war with Mexico in 1848, the Navajos were not particularly impressed. But when the United States Army arrived in force at the conclusion of the U.S. Civil War, matters took a grim turn for the Navajos. In a United States Army scorched-earth campaign led by Colonel Kit Carson, the Navajo homeland was devastated. Half of the Navajos, demoralized and starving, surrendered to the army and were marched 370 miles (592 kilometers) to eastern New Mexico to the Bosque Redondo internment camp on the Pecos River. There, many of them died, two thousand of them in one year alone from smallpox. After four years of imprisonment, in 1868, they were allowed to return to their homeland, now reduced to one-tenth its original size by the treaty of 1868. They began rebuilding their lives and their herds, virtually unnoticed in a land that most Americans considered worthless desert wasteland.

Today, the Navajo Nation is a country larger than the combined states of Massachusetts, New Hampshire, and Vermont. Its lands cover portions of three states: Arizona, New Mexico, and Utah. The Navajo Nation is the largest reservation-based Indian nation by far within the United States, both in land area and in population. More than two hundred thousand Navajos live on the 24,000 square miles (62,400 square kilometers) of the Navajo Nation.

The Navajo name for themselves is Dine, meaning "the people." Navajo is the name they were called by the Zunis and later by Spain, Mexico, and the United States. In 1969, the Navajo Tribal Council officially designated the nation the "Navajo Nation."

No tribe in North America has been more vigorously studied by anthropologists than the Navajos. When a man marries, he moves into the household of the wife's extended family. The Navajos say that a Navajo family consists of a grandmother, her married daughters and their spouses and children, and an anthropologist.

A Navajo is "born to" the mother's clan and "born for" the father's clan. The membership of each clan is dispersed throughout the nation. The importance of clans has gradually diminished in favor of the increasingly important role of the chapter house, which is based on the geographical proximity of its members. Traditional prohibitions against marrying within one's own clan are beginning to break down. The girl's puberty ceremony, her *kinaalda*, is a major event in Navajo family life.

Navajos maintain strong ties with relatives, even when they leave the reservation. It is not uncommon for Navajos working in urban centers to send money home to relatives. On the reservation, an extended family may have only one wage-earning worker. Other family members busy themselves with traditional endeavors, from stock tending to weaving. From the late 1860s until the 1960s, the local trading post was the preeminent financial and commercial institution for most Navajos, serving as a local bank (where silver and turquoise could be pawned), a post office, and a store. Traders served the community as interpreters, business managers, funeral directors, gravediggers, and gossip columnists. The automobile and big discount stores in the urban centers at the fringes of the Navajo Nation have greatly diminished the role of the trading posts. One of the most famous, Hubbell's Trading Post, is now a national monument.

A family on the Navajo Reservation in New Mexico eats fry bread in their hogan. Fry bread has become a popular food among Native and non-Native Americans alike, particularly at powwows and American Indian restaurants.

Under a sign welcoming Navajo soldiers home from Operation Desert Storm (the war in the Persian Gulf), the Navajo Nation Council convenes in April 1991.

The basic unit of local government in the Navajo Nation is the chapter, each with its own chapter house. The chapter system was created in 1922 as a means of addressing agricultural problems at a local level. The nation had no centrally organized tribal government before the 1920s. Like many other Indian nations, the tribe was forced to create a central authority by the United States. For the Navajos, the discovery of oil on the reservation in 1921 was crucial, since afterward the United States desired some centralized governmental authority for the Navajos to execute oil leases, largely for the benefit of non-Navajos. At first, the Bureau of Indian Affairs appointed three Navajos to execute mineral leases. In 1923, this arrangement gave way to a scheme for each of several Navajo agencies to provide representatives for the Navajo government. After World War II, the Navajo Tribal Council became recognized as the Navajo government.

The treaty of 1868 provided for schools for Navajo children, and the number of schools greatly increased after compulsory school attendance was mandated in 1887. In 1907, a Navajo headman in Utah was imprisoned without trial for a year and a half for speaking out against forced removal of local children to the Shiprock Boarding School. Others were strongly in favor of schools, especially after nineteen influential Navajo headmen were exposed to the outside world at the 1893 Columbian Exhibition in Chicago. Until 1896, the schools were operated by missionaries, who were frequently more interested in attempting to suppress the Navajo religion, culture, and language than in educating their charges. Because of great distances and few roads, boarding schools had to be established, which subjected children to the trauma of being removed from their families and their cultures for extended periods of time. Instruction was conducted only in English.

With changes in federal policy in 1896 regarding the Navajo public school system, civil servants replaced the missionaries. But lack of understanding and appreciation of Navajo culture—and instruction only in English—continued to be the norm. Some religious schools continue to the present day, but they display a greater appreciation for

Navajo culture and traditions than in the preceding century. By 1958, 93 percent of Navajo children were in school.

During the 1960s, Navajos began to exercise a much greater control over their children's education with the establishment of community-controlled contract schools. The Rough Rock Demonstration School was the first of these schools. It introduced bilingual education for young children, the training of adult Navajo medicine men, and other innovative programs based on the perceived needs of the local community.

In 1969, the Navajos established Navajo Community College, the first college operated by Indians. At first located at Many Farms High School, it moved to Tsaile, Arizona, with the opening of its new campus in 1974. Shiprock, New Mexico, has a branch campus of Navajo Community College. In 1972, the College of Ganado, a junior college in Ganado, Arizona, was incorporated as a successor to the Ganado Mission School. Following the lead of the Navajos, the United States today boasts a total of twenty-nine Indian institutions of higher education, all of them members of an American Indian higher education consortium. Navajo Community College Press is a leading Native-owned academic press. A number of state-supported four-year institutions are located nearby. These include branch campuses of the University of New Mexico at Gallup and Farmington, Northern Arizona University at Flagstaff, and Ft. Lewis College in Durango, Colorado. By the late 1980s, more than four thousand Navajos were attending college.

In the twentieth century, much friction has resulted between the Navajos and the United States over the management of Navajo livestock grazing. The original Navajo Reservation in 1868 encompassed only a small portion of the ancestral Navajo rangelands. The size of the reservation tripled between 1868 and the mid-1930s by additions of blocks of land in 1878, 1880, 1882, 1884, 1900, 1901, 1905, 1907, 1913, 1917, 1930, 1931, 1933,

These children, both members of the Tony Naki family, are at play outside their family home in Red Mesa, Utah, on the Navajo Reservation.

A rug-registration tag serves as both a certificate of authenticity and a greeting to tourists buying original Navajo crafts outside the confines of the Navajo Nation at Mesa Verde National Park, Colorado.

and 1934. This would give the appearance of a rapidly expanding amount of rangeland available to the Navajos. In fact, just the opposite was true.

When the Navajos had returned to their homeland from the Bosque Redondo, the government issued them one thousand goats and fourteen thousand sheep in 1869 to begin replacing their herds, which Kit Carson had either slaughtered or confiscated. In 1870, they were issued an additional ten thousand sheep. With practically no European-American encroachment on their ancestral rangeland, reservation boundaries had little meaning; the Navajos spread out over their old estate, and their herds began increasing. The Bureau of Indian Affairs forbade the selling of breeding stock, eager to see the Navajos regain self-sufficiency. Navajo population increased steadily, from an estimated ten to twelve thousand in 1868 to nearly forty thousand by 1930. Their herds increased accordingly, though there were large fluctuations in the numbers year by year due to occasional drought and disease.

At the same time, European-American cattle operations and other interests, increasingly and with gathering speed, appropriated the ancestral rangelands outside the reservation boundaries, forcing the Navajos onto an ever smaller amount of range. By the 1920s, a serious soil erosion problem on the reservation was being blamed on overgrazing. The Navajos sought to alleviate the problem by seeking more land and by seeking renewed access to the ancestral rangelands that had gradually been taken from them. The United States sought a solution to the problem by forcing Navajo livestock reductions: Animals it deemed to be unnecessary were killed. The government was indifferent to the importance of the animals in Navajo culture and did not even try to understand why each Navajo had to have so many sheep and horses. Thus began a twenty-year conflict between the Navajos and the United States.

The U.S. government, in attempting to implement its policies, found itself disrupting traditional Navajo economic, social, and political life to a

NAVAJO RESERVATION

The Navajo Nation is the largest reservation-based Indian nation within the United States, both in land area and in population. More than two hundred thousand Navajos live on the 24,000 square miles (62,400 square kilometers) of the Navajo Nation. Most of the nation lies in northeastern Arizona, but it also includes portions of northwestern New Mexico and southeastern Utah. It is a land of vast spaces and only a few all-weather roads. Many areas do not have electricity, and 88 percent of the reservation is without telephone service.

The local unit of Navajo government is called the chapter. There are more than one hundred chapter houses throughout the nation, which serve as local administrative centers for geographical regions. Before the 1990 tribal elections, the tribal council system of government was reorganized into executive, legislative, and judicial branches. In 1990, Navajos elected a tribal president for the first time, rather than a tribal chairman. The tribal budget exceeds $100 million annually, with much of the revenue coming from mineral leases.

As created by treaty in 1868, the reservation encompassed only about 10 percent of the ancestral Navajo homeland. The land base soon tripled in size, largely by the addition of large blocks of land by executive orders of presidents of the United States during the late nineteenth century, when non-Native Americans still considered most of the desert Southwest to be undesirable land. Dozens of small increments were also added by various methods until the middle of the twentieth century. The additions of land to the reservation occurred in 1878, 1880, 1882, 1884, 1900, 1901, 1905, 1907, 1913, 1917, 1930, 1931, 1933, and 1934. Navajos today are still adjusting the boundaries of their nation, trading land in some areas in an attempt to create contiguous blocks of land in an area of the nation outside the reservation called the Checkerboard.

Sheep herding on the Navajo Reservation. Like the land upon which the animals graze, the presence of livestock such as sheep and cattle have long been a vital element in Navajo life—a factor to which the U.S. government paid little attention when it embarked on its various policies to reduce the size of Navajo lands and herds.

Navajo silver for sale at the Gallup Flea Market on the Navajo Reservation in New Mexico. Turquoise has long been a popular style of jewelry among non-Indians, and many non-Native people from other parts of the world erroneously identify it as common to Native communities that are culturally and geographically distant from the Navajos.

The Checkerboard lies along the eastern boundary of the Navajo Nation. More than thirty thousand Navajos live in this 7,000-square-mile- (18,200-square-kilometer-) area of northwestern New Mexico. These Navajos are interspersed with Euro-American and Mexican stock raisers in a nightmare of legal tangles regarding title to the land, where there are fourteen different kinds of landownership. This problem originated in the nineteenth century when railroad companies were granted rights of way consisting of alternating sections of land. It was further complicated by the partial allotments of 160-acre (64-hectare) parcels of land to some individual Navajos, the reacquisition of some parcels by the federal government as public domain land, and other factors. Crownpoint is the Navajo administrative headquarters for the Checkerboard, the Eastern Navajo Agency. As recently as 1991, the Navajos were still attempting to consolidate the Checkerboard, exchanging 20,000 acres (8,000 hectares) in order to achieve 80,000 acres (32,000 hectares) of consolidated land.

There are three isolated portions of the nation in New Mexico, satellite reservations known as the Ramah Navajo, the Canoncito Navajo, and the Alamo Navajo. Canoncito was first settled about 1818. Ramah and Alamo had their origins in the late 1860s when some Navajos settled in these areas on their way back toward the Navajo homeland from imprisonment at the U.S. Army internment camp at Bosque Redondo in eastern New Mexico. Ramah is rural and is a bastion of traditional Navajo life. More than fifteen hundred Navajos live at Ramah, which is between the pueblos of Zuni and Acoma, near El Malpais National Monument. More than seventeen hundred Navajos live at Canoncito, which is to the east of Mt. Taylor, near the pueblos of Laguna and Isleta. More than two thousand Navajos live at Alamo, which is south of the pueblos of Acoma and Laguna.

Rounding up sheep on the Navajo Reservation in Utah.

Because they have remained relatively isolated from the centers of population, because they have been able to hold on to a large part of their ancestral homeland, and because of the great distances and poor roads within the region, Navajos have been more successful than most Native Americans in retaining their culture, language, and customs. Until early in this century, Navajos were also able to carry out their traditional way of life and support themselves with their livestock and still remain relatively unnoticed by the dominant culture. Boarding schools, the proliferation of automobiles and roads, and federal land management policies, especially regarding traditional Navajo grazing practices, have all made the reservation a different place than what it was a century ago. As late as 1950, paved roads ended at the fringes of the reservation, at Shiprock, Cameron, and Window Rock. Wagons were not even widely used until the early 1930s. By 1974, however, almost two-thirds of all Navajo households owned an automobile.

Navajos are finding ways to use some changes to support traditional culture, such as the adult education program at Navajo Community College that assists in teaching the skills that new Navajo medicine men must acquire in order to serve their communities. Bilingual education programs and broadcast and publishing programs in the Navajo language are also using the tools of change to preserve and strengthen traditional cultural values and language.

— D. L. Birchfield

SEE ALSO:
Bosque Redondo; General Allotment Act; Navajo; Navajo Community College.

NAVAJO URANIUM MINING

SEE Uranium Mining, Navajo.

NEBRASKA

The word *Nebraska* comes from the Sioux (some sources say Oto) language meaning "broad water" or "flat water," probably a reference to the Platte River before dams near its source drained most of its flow. Nebraska became the thirty-seventh U.S. state in 1867, but Native people have been living in the region for thousands of years. Today, four recognized Native groups—Poncas, Omahas (or U'ma'has), Winnebagos, and Santee Sioux—reside on reservations in Nebraska. A part of the Sac and Fox Reservation straddles the Nebraska border with Kansas.

The name of the largest city in Nebraska, Omaha, is an anglicized version of the name by which the original people in the same area called themselves. The Omahas, who reside on a small reservation sixty miles (ninety-seven kilometers) north of Omaha, near Macy, are the originators of the modern powwow format. Their small gathering in Macy is almost two hundred years old and has escaped the large number of tourists who attend some other powwows.

Prominent Native Americans from Nebraska include Susan Picotte-LaFlesche (Omaha), one of the first women to practice medicine in the nineteenth century, and Standing Bear (Ponca), who in 1879 won a ruling in Omaha federal court that, for the first time, said that Native Americans were to be treated as human beings under United States law.

The 1990 U.S. Census lists 12,410 American Indians living in Nebraska, ranking the state thirty-fifth in Native population.

SEE ALSO:
Omaha; Picotte-LaFlesche, Susan; Ponca; Powwow; Winnebago.

A group of Omaha Indians, some wearing U.S. Army apparel, pose outside their home in this photo taken in nineteenth-century Nebraska.

The origin of the dream catcher is unclear, though it is widely considered to be of Native origin. One purported purpose of this artifact, which has become popular among many non-Native Americans, is to trap bad dreams before they can descend into the sleep of the person who sleeps beneath it, allowing good dreams to filter through. Many Native people are concerned that by "adopting" Native ceremonial practices, many non-Native adherents of the New Age movement, while well-intentioned, diminish the significance of Native spirituality.

The problem for Native people with this appropriation of their ways is that often non-Natives begin to market, or profit from, artifacts or ceremonies that are ancient and sacred. Indeed, there is a growing industry selling Native American objects, from dream catchers to sacred herbs such as sage or sweet grass that are used to smudge (cleanse by bathing in smoke). At other times, non-Natives conduct rituals such as sweat lodges or pipe ceremonies that are based on Native ways but are not true to the Native spirit and usually performed in ignorance.

These practices are generally offensive to Native Americans. One of the reasons is that Native people hold their religious or spiritual leaders in high regard. Most states have laws prohibiting someone from impersonating a member of the clergy, because spiritual matters are very personal; it is understood that a certain process to ordain a person to preach or for a person to guide members of a congregation is required. Thus, when non-Natives attempt to play the role of a Native spiritual leader, it is offensive. Native people believe that their ways are being mocked or copied, no matter how well-intentioned the performer.

To add to the confusion, many Native communities are divided on the issue. Some members believe that sharing spiritual knowledge is a good thing to do if it will help create more respect for the planet and the environment. Others believe that once shared, the knowledge will be abused and used for profit by corporations or the so-called wannabees. *Wannabee* (a slang form of "want-to-be") is a term that describes a pretender, such as an individual with little or no Indian blood or lineage who claims to be Native, or desires to be, based on romantic notions or stereotypes.

The problem many Native Americans grapple with concerning the New Age movement is that it seems a pantomime of Indian ways by people who share little or no experience, history, culture, or community. The feeling is that so many people want to be Indian because of the effects of other cultural phenomena—such as the men's movement, the women's movement, multicultural awareness, books and movies, audio- and videotapes—that promote a longing to share with others or with the earth. The problem is that an individual cannot instantly become an Indian or teach Indian values, just as Native people cannot suddenly decide to turn their collars around and profess to "act" like a minister or impersonate a rabbi. Thus, the New Age movement poses many concerns for Native people, who generally feel that it is improper to "play Indian."

Like many involved in the New Age movement, Native American people, like other indigenous peoples around the world, feel that the environment is a major concern and that dominant cultures have done much to degrade the environment. To that end, many Native people are committed to providing insight into wise ways of being and thinking about our futures. However, there is also an understanding that the world's problems are not of Native making and that Native peoples do not have all the blueprints for a perfect world.

SEE ALSO:
Ceremonies, Exploitation of; Native American Awareness.

NEW BRUNSWICK

New Brunswick is one of the four original provinces of the Dominion of Canada, which was formed in 1867. The province is roughly rectangular in shape, with an area of 28,355 square miles (73,723 square kilometers). It is bounded on its western border by the U.S. state of Maine, on the north by the province of Quebec, to the east by the Gulf of St. Lawrence and the Northumberland Strait, and to the south by the Bay of Fundy. New Brunswick's largest town is St. John, and its capital is Fredericton.

New Brunswick has been home to Native peoples since the receding of the last Ice Age. At the time of European contact in the late fifteenth century, the land was inhabited by the Micmacs and Malecites, both Algonquian-language speakers. These tribes relied primarily on hunting and fishing for subsistence, although the Malecites did cultivate corn in the fertile St. John River Valley.

The Native peoples of New Brunswick were greatly affected by two historical events. The first was the expulsion of the French from North America in the mid-eighteenth century and the British takeover of Acadia, of which New Brunswick was a part. The second event was the influx of about fourteen thousand loyalist refugees fleeing into New Brunswick from the newly formed United States after the American Revolution. The British government forced Natives onto reserves to free up land for these new colonists.

There are currently twenty-five Native reserves in New Brunswick with a total acreage of 43,464 (17,386 hectares). The total Native population of New Brunswick exceeds twelve thousand. Because of the general poverty of rural New Brunswick, there is a great deal of movement of Native peoples back and forth between the reserves and the larger metropolitan areas, where there are more job and education opportunities.

SEE ALSO:
Algonquian; Canada, Native–Non-Native Relations in; Micmac.

NEWFOUNDLAND

Newfoundland, the easternmost province of Canada, comprises the island of Newfoundland and the mainland region of Labrador. Newfoundland joined the Canadian Union in 1949. Until it voted to join Canada, becoming its tenth province, Newfoundland had been a British colony. The province is bounded by Quebec on its west and south and has a total area of 156,649 square miles (407,287 square kilometers). The provincial capital is St. John's on the island of Newfoundland.

Newfoundland has been occupied by First Nations (Native or aboriginal) peoples for thousands of years. Many historians believe that the first European settlers in North America were Norse explorers who landed on the island of Newfoundland around 1000 C.E. At the time of contact with British and French fishermen who came to Newfoundland in the 1500s and established what would become the first permanent European presence in the region, the wooded interior of Labrador was home to the Montagnais in the south and the Naskapis in the north. Today, their combined nations are known as the Innu. Inuits also had settlements on the Labrador coast, and the island of Newfoundland was occupied by the Beothuk people.

This elderly Micmac woman was photographed in New Brunswick in the early 1900s. The Micmac and Malecite peoples were the primary cultures in New Brunswick prior to European contact in the 1600s.

The Native populations of Newfoundland decreased dramatically after European contact because of disease, alcoholism, and warfare. The Beothuks battled both the French and the English for three hundred years to protect their hunting and fishing grounds. By the early nineteenth century, they had nearly reached the point of extinction. The Beothuk Foundation, established in 1827, failed to find any survivors on Newfoundland.

According to the 1986 Canadian Census, there were 9,555 persons of aboriginal, or Native, origin living in Newfoundland. There are no reserves, but many Natives are concentrated in four or five villages on the northern coast of Labrador. The only Native presence on the island of Newfoundland is a Micmac settlement. Like other people in Newfoundland, Native people are more apt to live in poverty than residents of other provinces in Canada. In 1993, at the Innu settlement on Davis Inlet, off the coast of Labrador, six Innu children aged twelve to fourteen years attempted suicide by inhaling gasoline fumes in plastic bags. This tragic event called national attention to two poignant issues: the results of a loss of traditional lifestyle suffered by the Innus upon their removal by the government to a small island, and the larger issue of the generally poor living conditions existing for all First Nations peoples in Canada.

A portrait of Passaconaway, a Pennacook leader who lived in present-day New Hampshire from the mid-sixteenth to the mid-seventeenth centuries. He became a peace mediator between local Indians and English settlers.

See also:
Canada, Native–Non-Native Relations in; Inuit; Micmac; Montagnais-Naskapi; Norse Exploration.

NEW HAMPSHIRE

New Hampshire, one of the original thirteen colonies to form the United States, became the ninth U.S. state on June 21, 1788. It was the first of the colonies to form an independent government, which it did in 1776, six months before the signing of the Declaration of Independence. New Hampshire was also the first colony to sign the Declaration of Independence, which proclaimed the American colonies' independence from England.

The area that includes present-day New Hampshire has been home to Native peoples since well before the arrival of European colonizers. Central and southern New Hampshire, with its longer planting season and terrain hospitable to village life, is the historic home of several bands of the Western Abenakis. The Sokokis lived on both sides of the Connecticut River. Near Concord (the capital of New Hampshire) lived the Pennacooks. Others, such as the Amaskeags, Souhegans, and coastal Pawtuckets, also shared the region, which along with present-day Vermont was known to the Western Abenakis as Ndakinna, meaning "Our Land."

These Abenaki communities lived peacefully, hunting moose, bear, beaver, and occasional caribou in the high peaks of the White Mountains. Colonial records say little about diplomatic relations with Europeans in the state's present boundaries; conflicts and missionary activities largely occurred elsewhere. In the 1740s, however, Abenakis attacked English settlers who had violated a treaty prohibiting their expansion. Also in the 1700s, Abenaki peoples allied with the French during the Seven Years' War (called the French and Indian War in America); and after the American Revolution, in which they preferred neutrality, most relocated to Abenaki communities in Vermont and Odanak, Quebec. Even so, New Hampshire's original inhabitants have never relinquished family hunting grounds in the area.

In Hanover, New Hampshire, Dartmouth College was established in 1774 by Reverend Ebenezer Wheelock of Connecticut, with funds collected at home and in England by Samson Occom, his Mohegan protegé. Indians from eastern tribes, especially Abenakis, attended Dartmouth. Although there are no reservations in New Hampshire, isolated Pennacook and other Indian families still live in southern New Hampshire, and Dartmouth continues its commitment to educating Native Americans with over 150 enrolled annually.

The 1990 U.S. Census lists 2,136 Indians as New Hampshire residents, which ranks the state forty-eighth among states in Native American population.

SEE ALSO:
Abenaki; American Revolution; Connecticut; French and Indian War; Quebec; Vermont; Wabanaki Confederacy.

NEW JERSEY

New Jersey, one of the original thirteen colonies to form the United States, became the third U.S. state on December 18, 1787. Originally a part of the Dutch New Netherland colony, it was organized as an English colony in 1665, one year after the Dutch surrender to England turned New Netherlands into New York.

There is no colorful history of Indians in New Jersey as there is in neighboring states. New Jersey encompasses part of the vast homelands of the Lenape or Delaware Nation, an Algonquian group with several subdivisions, principally the Munsee, Unami, and Unalachtigo.

After losing their homeland to English, Dutch, and Swedish settlers by the early 1700s, the Lenapes were vulnerable to the losses of land, culture, and life that Native peoples suffered throughout the colonial era and into the establishment of the United States as an independent republic. Even the Lenapes' acculturation to European ways failed to prevent their impoverishment or protect them from white encroachments. By mid-century, numerous families began a westward migration that took them ultimately to Oklahoma and Ontario. Others ended up in Wisconsin or western New York. In 1758, the Brotherton reservation of "Praying Indians" was created in Burlington County, and the Treaty of Easton gave the English title over northern Lenape lands. Eventually, Brotherton declined, but the people answered a Stockbridge Mahican invitation to join their *Brothertown* community.

Several Lenape-based communities survive in New Jersey today. The Ramapough Mountain Indians are a collective of tribes who gathered in the hilly refuge along the New Jersey–New York border. Nearby European-American residents and scholars have tried to discredit the Indian identity of this group by proclaiming them to be "Jackson Whites," an alleged mulatto group (mixed Euro- and African-American) created during the American Revolution. Bridgeton, in Cumberland County, has a Lenape community that some Nanticokes from Delaware joined in the nineteenth century. Southeast of Trenton (the capital of New Jersey), a group of Lenape and Powhatan Indians have established the small Rancocus Reservation. At one time in Monmouth County, a Lenape and Cherokee community known as the Sand Hill Indians helped construct seashore resort sites.

Many New Jersey Indian families have relocated to metropolitan areas in order to find jobs. The New Jersey Indian Office and the American Indian Center are active organizations that promote communication and support among New Jersey Native Americans.

The 1990 U.S. Census lists 14,970 Indians as New Jersey residents, which ranks the state twenty-eighth among states in Native American population.

SEE ALSO:
American Revolution; Lenape; Munsee; New York.

NEW MEXICO

New Mexico became the forty-seventh U.S. state on January 6, 1912. American Indians have lived in the region of New Mexico for nine thousand years or longer, going back to Paleo-Indian times. In recent years, some archaeologists have pointed to evidence suggesting even longer Native occupation of the area (some say as far back as twenty thousand years ago). These findings have been a source of considerable controversy and debate, however, and many scientists consider the findings to be inaccurate or even fraudulent

From about 100 B.C.E. to 1300 C.E., the Anasazi culture flourished in New Mexico and in other locations in the Southwest. *Anasazi* is a Navajo word

The Salinas Archaeological Site in New Mexico. This site, with ruins showing evidence of indigenous Pueblo and early Spanish settlement, was abandoned in the 1670s.

A young man stands beside a poster from the Picuris Pueblo Museum during a harvest ceremony at San Ildefonso Pueblo, New Mexico.

that means "ancient ones." At times, *Anasazi* has been inaccurately translated as "ancient enemies." In the northwest corner of New Mexico, the Anasazi ruins at Chaco Canyon have been extensively excavated and studied. The largest Anasazi site at Chaco Canyon, Pueblo Bonito, was named a national monument in 1907. In 1980, the site was renamed the Chaco Canyon Culture National Historic Park.

By the late 1300s, the Anasazi culture was in decline. Tree-ring evidence indicates that a great drought had taken place in the region from 1276 C.E. to 1299 C.E. Some archaeologists argue that this drought, along with famine and disease, caused the decline in the Anasazi culture. Other archaeologists argue that conflict may have split the Ansazis into warring factions, and this resulted in the decline.

For many years, the archaeologists who studied the Anasazis stated that the Anasazi culture "vanished" around 1300 C.E. Most current archaeologists studying the Anasazi now believe that the Pueblo cultures—such as the Hopis, Zunis, and Rio Grande Pueblos—are descendants of the Anasazis.

The first Europeans who visited New Mexico were the survivors of the Narvaez expedition, including Alvar Núñez Cabeza de Vaca. Another Spanish explorer, Marcos de Niza, saw the Zuni villages in New Mexico in 1539, although he never was able to enter them. He falsely described the villages as "the Seven Golden Cities of Cibola." In 1540, Francisco Vásquez de Coronado seized the Zuni pueblo at Hawikuh, but he found no gold there or at any other of the Zuni towns.

The Spanish colonized New Mexico in 1598, establishing San Juan Pueblo. The Spanish rule of the Pueblo people was very cruel, and in 1680, the Pueblos staged a revolt and forced the Spanish out of the area for nearly fifteen years.

In addition to the Pueblo cultures, the Spanish also fought with the Ute, Navajo, and Apache peoples in New Mexico. Indian resistance to Mexican and U.S. rule continued until 1886, when the Apache leaders Geronimo and Juh finally surrendered.

Currently, many reservations exist in New Mexico. They include Acoma Pueblo, Alamo, Canoncito, Cochiti Pueblo, Isleta Pueblo, Jemez Pueblo, Jicarilla Apache, Laguna Pueblo, Mescalero Apache, Nambe Pueblo, Picuris Pueblo, Pojoaque Pueblo, Ramah Community, Sandia Pueblo, San Felipe Pueblo, San Ildefonso Pueblo, San Juan Pueblo,

Santa Ana Pueblo, Santa Clara Pueblo, Santa Domingo Pueblo, Taos Pueblo, Tesuque Pueblo, Zia Pueblo, and Zuni Pueblo. The reservations range in size from Pojoaque Pueblo's 1,842 acres (737 hectares) to Jicarilla Apache with 823,580 acres (329,432 hectares).

The 1990 U.S. Census lists 134,355 Indians as New Mexico residents, ranking the state fourth in terms of Native American population.

SEE ALSO:
Acoma Pueblo; Anasazi; Apache; Cabeza de Vaca, Alvar Núñez; Chaco Canyon; Coronado Expedition; De Niza, Marcos; Geronimo; Hopi; Isleta Pueblo; Jicarilla Apache; Juh; Mescalero Apache; Navajo; New Spain; Pueblo; Pueblo Revolt of 1680; Spain; Taos Pueblo; Zuni.

A bike, a boom box, and a Bears football jersey give a clue to the interests of these boys at San Ildefonso Pueblo.

NEW SPAIN

New Spain (more properly "The Viceroyalty of New Spain"—*Virreinato de Nueva España*) was the name of several administrative districts that Spain created to govern conquered and colonized areas of North and Central America. First established in 1535, New Spain included what is now Mexico and Central America (excluding Panama, which was part of the viceroyalty of New Granada. Later, present-day California and New Mexico were added. New Spain later came to include points along the Gulf Coast into Florida. The islands of the Caribbean that Spain colonized also were part of New Spain. In 1565, even the Philippine Islands were placed under the administrative direction of the viceroyalty of New Spain.

During the first century of Spanish rule in New Spain, the Native American population of the area declined from about twenty-five million to one million because of disease, maltreatment, and war. The Spanish ranged well into the present-day area of the United States during the early years of the viceroyalty; they even established a small fort a few miles (several kilometers) south of present-day Omaha, Nebraska.

The population of New Spain assumed a mestizo (mixed Native American and European, primarily Spanish) composition after the Spanish conquest. The number of Spaniards who migrated to the so-called New World was not large (about three hundred thousand people over a century), and the majority of them were single men. Survivors of the diseases and violence that decimated the Native peoples frequently married the Span-

A store selling Southwest-style arts and crafts in Santa Fe, once a capital of New Spain, later the capital of the territory of New Mexico, and today the capital of the state of New Mexico. Scenes like this typify the mix of Spanish and Native influences in the region that was once part of the Spanish colonial empire known as New Spain.

ish. Today, most of the population of Mexico and a substantial portion of people in the southwestern states of the United States are of mixed Spanish and Indian heritage.

The colonization of large parts of the Americas by Spain had three primary missions. One aim was religious: The ideology of the Roman Catholic Church traveled with the soldiers of the Spanish state, and each new territory was claimed in the name of the Christian god, as well as the king of Spain. The second aim was political, to establish Spain as a world power and, most importantly, the main agent of global trade and commerce. The third major individual drive among the people who colonized New Spain was the possibility of discovering huge troves of gold that could make an individual wealthy for the rest of his life.

Ironically, the importation of so much gold and other treasure into Spain also fueled inflation in the Spanish economy and deepened class differences among Spaniards. More than 95 percent of the people found their incomes shrinking, as the upper 5 percent reveled in newfound wealth. Near the end of the sixteenth century, a commentator in Madrid described a woman of wealth picking her way through the sleeping destitute on the streets of Madrid. One major beneficiary of New Spain's treasures was the port of Seville, which drew fortune hunters from all over the Iberian (Spanish-Portuguese) Peninsula. The city quickly grew to 150,000 people, making it one of the largest urban areas in Europe. At the same time, many villages in northern Spain, particularly in Galicia, were nearly depopulated.

The importation of treasure from New Spain increased from 445,266 ducats (a Spanish monetary measure) between 1503 and 1505 to more than 10 million ducats a year in the last years of the 1500s. The priest Bartolomé de Las Casas wrote of the cruelties inflicted on the Native peoples of Mexico and other provinces of New Spain in the search for treasures that made people rich in Spain. Las Casas wrote that some Indians were forced into pearl diving. "It is impossible to continue for so long diving into the cold water and holding the breath for minutes at a time . . . sun rise to sun set, day after day. They die spitting blood . . . looking like sea wolves or monsters of another species."

Some of the colonies under the administration of New Spain were founded as private enterprises. Juan de Oñate, for example, financed the founding of the first large colony in New Mexico himself. Having financed the colony and having found no appreciable gold or silver, Oñate and other governors after him tried to recoup their investments by demanding increasing amounts of tribute from Native peoples. Spanish priests also whipped Pueblo holy men to death in public to discourage what they regarded as "devil worship." The exploitation of the Pueblos and other Native peoples by the Spanish played a major role in setting off the Pueblo Revolt of 1680.

In 1821, the viceroyalty of New Spain was overthrown by advocates of Mexican independence. Mexico briefly annexed Central America, but new nations also emerged there by 1823, and Spain's presence in the Americas was further diminished by independence movements throughout Central America and the Caribbean.

— B. E. Johansen

SEE ALSO:
Aztec; California; Caribbean, Indigenous Cultures of; Catholic Church in the Spanish Empire; Central America, Indigenous Peoples of; Encomienda; Epidemic Diseases; Florida; Las Casas, Bartolomé de; Latinos; Maya; Mexico, Indigenous Peoples of; New Mexico; Oñate Expedition; Pueblo; Pueblo Revolt of 1680; Spain.

NEW YORK

New York, one of the original thirteen colonies to form the United States, became the eleventh U.S. state on July 26, 1788. Originally the Dutch New Netherland colony, it became New York in 1664 when the English took colonial possession.

No state outside of New England encountered greater resistance by Indians during the colonial era than New York, and among eastern states, none encountered Indian diplomacy as sophisticated as that experienced in New York. The Iroquois are dynamic leaders, whose Great Law of Peace continues to guide their spiritual, cultural, and political traditions. Their several reservations are small reminders of vast homelands and political power.

Two Algonquian peoples, the Mahicans and the Munsees, lived along the Hudson Valley and in the Catskill Mountains. The Manahattoes' sale of their island to the Dutch is legendary. Of the Native peoples throughout Long Island, there remain Matinecock families near Great Neck; the Montauks on the east end; and two state reservations, Unkechaug or Poosepatuck in Mastic, and Shinnecock in the resort town of Southampton. The Shinnecocks have hosted an annual powwow, which is well attended by Natives and non-Natives alike, since 1946. Eastern Long Island's peoples are traditionally seafaring, and in past years sailed across Long Island Sound to trade with the Narragansetts and other Native peoples in New England. They were expert whalers, and fishing and oyster cultivation have aided self-sufficiency at Shinnecock's shore, where property is highly valued by real estate agents and buyers. Along the state's border with New Jersey are the Ramapough Mountain Indians. The Iroquois actively pursue land claims in Albany, the capital of New York. And in 1993, Mohawks established Kanatsiohareke, a traditional community near Fonda.

New York City has long attracted Indian families, notably Iroquois, with work opportunities in high-steel construction projects such as the World Trade Center. Indians have long participated in the city's cultural life and promote their own organizations like American Indian Community House. An estimated twenty thousand reside in the five boroughs that make up New York City. Indian leaders from throughout the Americas periodically journey to address the United Nations as representatives of sovereign nations regarding issues of racism and Native American survival.

The 1990 U.S. Census lists 62,651 Indians as New York residents, which ranks the state ninth among states in Native American population.

SEE ALSO:
Algonquian; American Revolution; Iroquois Confederacy; Mohawk; "Mohawks in High Steel"; Munsee; Narragansett; New Jersey.

Stephen Scott, an Oneida Indian, dances at a competition in New York State. Along with other members of the Iroquois Confederacy, the Oneidas have long been a major cultural presence in the area now known as New York.

NEZ PERCE

Nez Perce (English pronounciation *NEZ-PURSE* and also spelled Nez Percé) is a term meaning "pierced nose." The French used this term to describe a number of tribes they thought pierced their noses for ornamental purposes. The term came to be used solely to identify the tribe that bears the name today—the Nez Perce, who have never to anyone's knowledge actually pierced their noses as a group as a form of artistic, decorative, or cultural expression.

The Nez Perce, also known as the Sahaptins, are members of the Shahaptian language family. Their presence in the Pacific Northwest predates by centuries the year 1805, which is when European explorers first happened upon them living in parts of present-day Idaho, Oregon, and Washington State.

The Nez Perce became steadfast United States allies as settlers moved into the Pacific Northwest in the face of opposition from Great Britain. They even rescued a group of U.S. troops in 1858. At about that same time, however, the United States signed a treaty with Nez Perce "treaty commissioners" who did not represent the nation. The treaty gave up the Nez Perce's Wallowa Valley to the United States, opening it for settlement. Chief Joseph (father of Young Joseph, whose long march with his people subsequently became legendary) protested that the treaty was illegal, a violation of another one signed only three years earlier.

The Nez Perce in Joseph's band stayed in the valley, despite the treaty. They tended their large herds of prize horses as settlers moved in around them, sparking several violent incidents. In 1871, Joseph senior died, and the leadership of his band passed to Hin-mah-too-yah-laht-ket,

This undated lithograph shows a group of Nez Perce gathered around a Euro-American visitor. The historical relationship between the Nez Perce and the U.S. government has been a mixture of cooperation and conflict.

A photographic portrait of Chief Joseph of the Nez Perce, taken in the late 1800s. Chief Joseph was praised by U.S. officers not only for his military prowess but for the care he took to avoid hurting innocent settlers.

whom English-speakers at first called Young Joseph and later Chief Joseph. Government emissaries continued to press the Nez Perce to move out of the valley to a reservation where they would be allocated too little land for each head of a household (defined in the European sense) to run the prized blue Appaloosa horses that they had developed and used for hunting and war.

Under pressure from the United States, in 1871, Joseph and his band signed the last treaty negotiated by any Native nation with the U.S. government. Under the terms of the treaty, the Nez Perce agreed to move to Lapwai, Idaho. As the logistics of the move were being worked out, settlers stole hundreds of the Nez Perce's prized horses. A renegade band of young Nez Perce retaliated by killing eighteen settlers, and the army was brought in to corral the "hostiles," sending the entire band, about five hundred men, women, and children, into the mountains.

During the next several months, the vastly outnumbered Nez Perce led troops on a 1,000-mile (1,610-kilometer) trek through some of the most rugged country on the continent, north into Canada, then south again. Joseph, with at most two hundred warriors, fought over a dozen engagements with four army columns, evading capture every time. On one occasion, in a night raid, the Nez Perce made off with the pursuing army's pack animals. At other times, the Nez Perce so skillfully evaded army pincer movements that the two closing columns ran into each other without capturing a single Indian. The army inflicted casualties on the Nez Perce at other times; eighty-nine were killed in one battle, fifty of them women and children.

Despite the deaths, the Nez Perce continued to fight. Chief Joseph instructed his warriors not to take scalps. The Nez Perce also earned praise for their military wisdom and skill from General William Tecumseh Sherman, who said the Indians went to great lengths to avoid killing innocent settlers. General Nelson A. Miles, whose army brought the Nez Perce's long march to an end, agreed with Sherman's opinion: "In this skillful campaign, they have spared hundreds of lives and thousands of dollars' worth of property that they might have destroyed."

Through the Bitterroot Mountains and what is now Yellowstone National Park, to the headwaters of the Missouri River, to the Bear Paw Mountains, Joseph's band fought a rear-guard action with unquestioned brilliance. Exhausted, the Nez Perce surrendered October 5, 1877, at Eagle Creek, roughly thirty miles (forty-eight kilometers) south of the Canadian border. Many of the Nez Perce were starving. Several were also maimed and blind. Joseph handed his rifle to General Miles and said he was "tired of fighting. . . . My people ask me for food, and I have none to give. It is cold, and we have no blankets, no wood. My people are starving to death. Where is my little daughter? I do not know. Perhaps, even now, she is freezing to death. Hear me, my chiefs. I have fought, but from where the sun now stands, Joseph will fight no more forever."

Chief Joseph then drew his blanket over his face and walked into the army camp, a prisoner. Of roughly 650 Nez Perce who had begun the long march, only 50 remained at its end.

After the surrender, Joseph and his band were marched to Indian Territory (present-day Oklahoma). In 1885, with only a few dozen people surviving, Joseph and his people were allowed to march northwest again, not to their home valley, but to northern Washington State. The Nez Perces were provided no supplies as they arrived at the onset of winter. They experienced profound suffering. A Lieutenant Wood, who had witnessed Chief Joseph's surrender speech and later wrote a narrative of the Nez Perces' long march, said, "I think that, in his long career, Joseph cannot accuse the Government of the United States of one single act of justice."

Today, the Nez Perce Reservation in Lapwai, Idaho, which is close to the borders of Washington and Oregon, is the site of numerous powwows and other tribal events.

— B. E. Johansen

SEE ALSO:
Chief Joseph; Idaho.

SUGGESTED READINGS:

Beal, Merrill D. *I Will Fight No More Forever*. Seattle: University of Washington Press, 1963.

Chalmers, Harvey. *The Last Stand of the Nez Perce*. New York: Twayne, 1962.

Chief Joseph. "An Indian's View of Indian Affairs." *North American Review*, 128 (April, 1879): 415–433.

Davis, Russell, and Brant Ashabranner. *Chief Joseph: War Chief of the Nez Perce*. New York: McGraw-Hill, 1962.

DeVoto, Bernard. *Across the Wide Missouri*. Cambridge: Harvard University Press, 1947.

Howard, Helen A., and Dan L. McGrath. *War Chief Joseph*. Caldwell, ID: Caxton, 1952.

Jackson, Helen Hunt. *A Century of Dishonor*. Boston, 1887.

Josephy, Alvin M. *The Nez Perce Indians and the Opening of the Northwest*. New Haven: Yale University Press, 1965.

Josephy, Alvin, Jr. *The Patriot Chiefs*. New York: Viking, 1961.

Lavender, David. *Let Me Be Free*. San Francisco: HarperCollins, 1992.

Nabokov, Peter. *Native American Testimony*. New York: Viking, 1991.

Waters, Frank. *Brave Are My People*. Santa Fe, NM: Clear Light, 1993.

NIATUM, DUANE (1938–)

Born in Seattle, Washington, on February 13, 1938, Duane Niatum is a writer of mixed descent—Italian and Klallam —and a member of the Jamestown band, S'Klallam tribe. His early life was spent in Washington, Oregon, California, Alaska, and Japan. After attending college at the University of Washington, he received his masters of arts degree from Johns Hopkins University. In the 1990s, he began working on his Ph.D. in cooperation with the University of Michigan.

ernments that have no desire to share their powers with the governments of Indian nations.

— D. L. Birchfield

SEE ALSO:
American Revolution; Choctaw; Oklahoma; Proclamation of 1763; Removal Act, Indian; Self-determination; Self-determination Policy.

NORTHWEST TERRITORIES

The Northwest Territories encompass 1,322,910 square miles (3,439,566 kilometers) across the top of Canada. They reach into the Arctic Circle and include the Arctic and sub-Arctic Native culture areas. Nearly half the population of the territories are First Nations peoples (Natives or aboriginals). Most of Canada's Inuit live in the Northwest Territories; the other Native people living there are from the Athabascan language family and now call themselves, collectively, the Dene. The tribal groups comprising the Dene are the Chipewyans, Beavers, Slaveys, Dogribs, and Yellowknives, among others. Because of the inhospitable nature of the land and its limited use for agriculture, the Native peoples of the Northwest Territories suffered fewer invasions by white settlers and were able to maintain their traditional lifestyles for much longer than other Canadian Natives.

The Inuit reside in the Arctic area of the Northwest Territories. They have at least nine distinct cultural groups, but all of them share the Inuktitut language and the nomadic lifestyle of hunting and fishing for food. The Inuit became dependent upon the fur trade, and their focus on fur trapping to the exclusion of traditional hunting activities created serious problems upon the collapse of the fur trade in the 1940s. This triggered a general movement into government housing settlements during the next decade. In the 1960s, the discovery of oil in the Arctic region further threatened Inuit culture and autonomy and resulted in the organization of several advocacy groups. These groups worked to settle land claims with the Canadian government. The Inuit have never lived on reserves, but they reside today in some forty-six communities scattered across the Arctic.

The tribal groups known today as the Dene Nation originally existed as mobile hunting, fishing, and gathering societies. The northern people depended heavily upon the caribou for food and clothing; the southern people likewise used the buf-

With his son curled up beside him, David Irngaut talks on the radio to other Inuit hunters from his summer camp in the Northwest Territories, Canada. Most Inuits live in the Arctic regions of the Northwest Territories.

falo for a variety of purposes. Their primary source of transportation was the birch-bark canoe in the summer; snowshoes and toboggans helped them get around in the winter. Again, mineral resource development of the region brought an influx of non-Natives and a different way of life. In 1975, the Dene Declaration was issued, stating the Dene Nation's right of self-determination.

Today, the Northwest Territories contains only two Indian reserves totaling approximately 33,500 acres (13,400 hectares). Fewer than one thousand First Nations people live on the reserves; about 35,000 live off-reserve in the territories, representing about 48 percent of the entire population in the province.

SEE ALSO:
Canada, Native–Non-Native Relations in; Inuit.

An Inuit couple discuss their purchases at a general store in Igloolik, Northwest Territories.

NOVA SCOTIA

Nova Scotia is one of the four original provinces of the Dominion of Canada, which was established in 1867. It comprises an area of 21,425 square miles (55,705 square kilometers) and includes the peninsula of Nova Scotia, Cape Breton Island, and other smaller islands off the coast. According to 1991 census figures, its population is 899,942, and Halifax is the provincial capital.

What archaeological evidence there is suggests that Nova Scotia has been continuously inhabited by aboriginal people (Natives or First Nations people) for thousands of years. At the time of European contact, the area was home to the Micmac Indians. The Micmacs were a seasonally nomadic people who had adjusted well to their physical environment. Winter months were spent in small family units at traditional hunting grounds in the interior. During the summer months, they would gather in larger bands along the coast to fish.

Politically, the Micmacs sided with the French during the French and English wars of the seventeenth and eighteenth centuries, but the victorious English took over what was then called Acadia in 1713. The traditional way of life changed greatly for the Micmacs with the end of the American Revolution and the sudden influx of loyalist colonists fleeing the United States into Nova Scotia. The demand for land by these loyalists and other immigrants from the British Isles resulted in the British government moving the Micmacs onto reserves.

There are currently about thirty-eight Native reserves in Nova Scotia encompassing about 28,300 acres (11,320 hectares). They are administered by thirteen tribal associations. The total Native population of Nova Scotia exceeds twenty thousand, with about fourteen thousand of those living off reserves. Through their tribal associations, the Micmacs continue to struggle to have their rights honored and respected. A 1985 Canadian Supreme Court decision upheld treaty rights in Nova Scotia, strengthening the Micmacs' position in their ongoing negotiations with the Nova Scotian government.

SEE ALSO:
Canada, Native–Non-Native Relations in; French and Indian Wars; Micmac.

located in both the United States and Canada, and by the eighteenth century, their tribe's land extended from the Great Lakes region to the Great Plains near present-day Lake Winnipeg in Manitoba and the Turtle Mountains in North Dakota. Today, the Ojibwe homelands include reservations in Michigan, Wisconsin, Minnesota, North Dakota, and Montana, as well as reserves in Ontario, Manitoba, and Saskatchewan. Other Ojibwes live in communities that have not received official or government recognition or in other off-reservation locales. The combined population of Ojibwes in the United States and Canada is estimated at over two hundred thousand.

The Ojibwes continue to engage in traditional, land-based cultural and economic pursuits, including fishing, hunting, and gathering, on both ceded and unceded lands. They have also developed new enterprises, such as local businesses and gaming establishments, to help sustain the people. The Lac Courte Oreilles Band, for example, owns a cranberry marsh, sawmill, and power plant. The reservation also has a radio station, newspaper, supermarket, and schools. Tribal colleges have been developed at Bay Mills in Michigan, Fond du Lac in Minnesota, Lac Courte Oreilles in Wisconsin, Rocky Boy in Montana, and Turtle Mountain in North Dakota. The tribal language, once forbidden in mission and government schools, is now taught in many communities. The Ojibwes are working to recover land, to reclaim language and traditions, and to rebuild communities after the devastating assimilation policies and practices of the past.

The following paragraphs offer a closer look at the various Ojibwe communities throughout the United States and Canada.

Michigan Ojibwe

Michigan Ojibwe groups include Keweenaw Bay Indian Community, Lac Vieux Desert Band of Lake Superior Chippewa, Bay Mills Indian Community, Sault Ste. Marie Tribe of Chippewa, the Saginaw Band of Chippewa, the Grand Traverse Band of Ottawa and Chippewa Indians, and the Burt Lake Ottawa and Chippewa. The Upper Peninsula groups (Keweenaw Bay, Lac Vieux Desert, Bay Mills, and Sault Ste. Marie) and the Saginaw Chippewa established tribal governments under the Wheeler-Howard Act of 1934 (also known as the Indian Reorganization Act or Indian New Deal). In the 1970s, Chippewas and Ottawas successfully pursued claims before the Indian Claims Commission, resulting in the reestablishment of governmental rights for the Grand Traverse Ottawa and Chippewa in 1980. The Burt Lake Ottawa and Chippewa are seeking restoration of the same rights through the claims process. It was not until 1991 that the United States government recognized the Lac Vieux Desert Chippewa as a tribal group separate from the Keweenah Bay Indian Community.

Wisconsin

Six Ojibwe reservations in Wisconsin are located in the northern area of the state. These reservations, which are part of the Southwestern Chippewa and form the Lake Superior Tribe of Chippewa, are Bad River, Lac Courte Oreilles, Lac du Flambeau, Red Cliff, St. Croix, and Sokaogon (Mole Lake). Four of the reservations—Bad River, Lac Courte Oreilles, Lac du Flambeau, and Red Cliff—were established under the Treaty of 1854. The remaining two were established by the secretary of the Department of the Interior in 1938.

In 1983, when off-reservation treaty rights were reaffirmed by the United States Court of Appeals through the Voigt Decision (*Lac Courte Oreilles Band, etc. v. Voigt,*), non-Indian protesters demonstrated against the Ojibwe. The Voigt Decision affirmed that the tribal group had reserved the right to hunt, fish, and gather on lands ceded or relinquished through treaties made with the federal government. Boat landings in the ceded area became the scene of violent confrontations as well-organized anti-Indian protesters sought to prevent Ojibwe spearfishers from exercising their rights. Using racial slurs such as "timber nigger," "spear an Indian, save a walleye," and "spear a pregnant squaw, save two walleye," these protesters formed antitreaty organizations, including Protect America's Rights and Resources (PARR) and Stop Treaty Abuse (STA). Tactics of members of these organizations included rock throwing, a propaganda campaign against the Ojibwes, and threats of violence and death against spearfishers.

The Voigt Decision resulted in a series of court cases, the mobilization of support on behalf of treaty rights, and the establishment of the Great Lakes Indi-

An undated artist's representation of a group of Ojibwes repairing a canoe. The historic ties of the Ojibwe, or Chippewa, people to land and water are reflected in their efforts to assert their tribal hunting and fishing rights.

an Fish and Wildlife Commission (GLIFWC). Member tribes include the six Wisconsin Ojibwe reservations, Fond du Lac and Mille Lacs Reservations in Minnesota, and Keweenaw Bay Indian Community, Bay Mills Indian Community, and Lac Vieux Desert Band of Lake Superior Chippewa Indians in Michigan. This intertribal resource management agency was formed to implement off-reservation treaty rights of hunting, fishing, and gathering. GLIFWC's programs include biological services, public information, conservation enforcement, intergovernmental affairs, and natural resource planning and development. Each tribal band maintains its own natural resource programs and conservation regulations to manage hunting, fishing, and gathering on and off reservation.

Minnesota

Ojibwe reservations in Minnesota include Bois Forte (Nett Lake), Fond du Lac, Grand Portage, Leech Lake, Mille Lacs, and White Earth. These six groups, which are located in the northern part of the state, form the Minnesota Chippewa Tribe (MCT). Red Lake, the seventh Ojibwe reservation in the state, is described separately below.

The MCT reservations were all established through nineteenth-century treaties with the U.S. government. Bois Forte, which ceded land in the La Pointe Treaty of 1854, was established by treaty in 1866. Additional land was added to the reservation in 1881 (Lake Vermilion) and in 1883 (Deer Creek). Fond du Lac, which is located twenty-five miles (forty kilometers) from Duluth, and Grand Portage, in the northeast, were both established in 1854. Leech Lake, established in 1864, ceded lands in the area through an earlier treaty (1855) between the Pillager and Lake Winnibigoshish Bands and the government. The Mille Lacs Reservation in central Minnesota was established in 1855. The White Earth Reservation in the northwestern part of the state was created by treaty in 1867.

Each reservation is governed locally by a tribal council, with the Minnesota Chippewa Tribe (MCT) representing member groups as a consolidated body. The constitution and bylaws of the MCT were ratified in 1936. The tribal headquarters of the Minnesota Chippewa Tribe is located on Cass Lake on the Leech Lake Reservation. In 1993, the MCT's tribal enrollment was cited at forty thousand.

Efforts to rebuild communities and revitalize tribal ways include the establishment of the White Earth Land Recovery Project at White Earth to address the massive land losses of previous centuries, the construction of a new community college building at Fond du Lac, the teaching of tribal language, culture, and history, and the development of both traditional and new business enterprises. Treaty rights are an important aspect of the struggle for self-determination and revitalization. The Mille Lacs Band, for example, filed suit in 1990 to have its treaty rights upheld. In 1994, U.S. District Court Chief Judge Diana Murphy upheld the treaty rights of the Mille Lacs Band to hunt, fish, and gather on ceded lands. Phase II of the litigation, scheduled to begin in the fall of 1996, will determine the extent of the right and the extent, if any, of state regulation.

The seventh and largest Anishinabe reservation in Minnesota is Red Lake, which extends over 550,000 acres (220,000 hectares) and is located south of Lake of the Woods and approximately thirty-five miles (fifty-six kilometers) from the town of Bemidji. Two large lakes, Upper Red Lake and Lower Red Lake, account for more than one-third of Red Lake's acreage. The band is known for its successful resistance to outside encroachment on tribal lands and traditions. While some territory was ceded through treaties or agreements signed in 1864, 1889, and 1904, Native lands surrounding Lower Red Lake and part of Upper Red Lake were not relinquished. Red Lake successfully opposed nineteenth-century allotment policies, such as the Nelson Act in Minnesota. The band also maintained its political independence, opposing the Indian Reorganization Act of 1934 and remaining separate when the other Ojibwe reservations in the state incorporated as the Minnesota Chippewa Tribe. Today's enterprises include a fishery association, which was established in 1929. In 1993, Red Lake's tribal membership was cited at 7,940.

North Dakota

The Turtle Mountain Reservation, which was established in 1882, is the only Ojibwe reservation in North Dakota. Located in the north-central part of the state, it represents North Dakota's smallest tribal land base and largest tribal population. Today's tribal members are descendants of the Anishinabegs who extended their territory from the eastern Great Lakes region to the northern Great Plains in the seventeenth century. There, they became known as the Plains Ojibwe or Bungi (Bungee) Ojibwe, adjusting to their new environment by adopting ways suited to the region.

While maintaining aspects of their original woodland culture, they also engaged in cultural practices associated with other Plains peoples. Thus, the Plains Ojibwes adopted the Sun Dance, lived in tipis, and hunted buffalo. This tribal population, which included Ojibwes, Crees, and Métis (mixed-bloods) or Mitchifs (also Michifs) engaged in hunting, trapping, and trading in the region. When the international boundary between the United States and Canada was established, the tribal land base and legal status of tribal group members were adversely affected. Pembina, which was once a part of Rupert's Land or Assiniboia in present-day Canada and the heart of Plains Ojibwes' and Métis' territory, became part of the United States. The tribal people were classified as American or Canadian by government officials, creating complications for those who continued to travel back and forth across the border to visit relatives and to follow traditional subsistence patterns. Many people, for instance, spent part of the time in North Dakota, Montana, and in the Canadian provinces of Manitoba and Saskatchewan before settling on or near a reservation.

Historical events affecting the Ojibwes in today's North Dakota included the establishment of the reservation by executive order in 1882. Twenty-two townships in present-day Rolette County were set aside by presidential executive order for a homeland for the Turtle Mountain Band of Chippewa. Two years later, the federal government reduced the reservation to two townships or 46,080 acres (18,432 hectares), concluding that most of the Métis were Canadian. Although a third executive order amended the township designations, it did not restore land to the reservation.

Under the leadership of Chief Little Shell, the Turtle Mountain people sought to have their original reservation lands restored, disenfranchised relatives reenrolled, and just compensation for the group's ten-million-acre (four-million-hectare) land claim. The Agreement of 1892, which was ratified as the Agreement of 1904, finally provided one million dollars in payment for tribal land. This settlement became known as the "ten cent treaty" for its ten cents per acre compensation. The land base of Turtle Mountain Band members was further reduced by allotment policies during the period.

The population at Turtle Mountain numbered approximately ten thousand by the early 1990s, with a total tribal enrollment of over twenty-five thousand.

An undated portrait of an Ojibwe man identified as "Okee-Makee-Quid, a Chippeway Chief."

Montana

Montana's Ojibwe groups include the Rocky Boy Chippewa-Cree, the Little Shell Band of Chippewa, Landless Chippewa, and the Turtle Mountain Allotment Community. Most of the Ojibwe population in what is now Montana originated with the Pembina Band of Chippewa of the Red River Valley, covering a range of territory that became divided by the establishment of the international boundary between the United States and Canada. Woodland Ojibwes, Crees, and Métis or Mitchifs migrated to the area of present-day Montana, adopting cultural aspects of the Great Plains region while maintaining aspects of their earlier woodland ways.

Each of the Montana Ojibwe groups is described in further detail in the paragraphs that follow.

Rocky Boy Chippewa-Cree. Following the failed attempt by Métis leader Louis Riel to create a separate state in present-day Canada in 1868, about four thousand Pembina Band Chippewa-Cree moved onto land in what is now Montana. By the early 1880s, however, United States officials began rounding up tribal people they considered Canadian and forcing them into Canada. Eventually, many deported Ojibwes and Métis returned to Montana to live.

In 1885, when Louis Riel's followers again failed in their resistance against the Canadian government, Ojibwe leader Stone Child, or Rocky Boy, led a number of his followers into Montana. Some Métis joined the group, while others migrated to present-day Lewistown, Montana. Rocky Boy and his followers were joined by Cree leader Little Bear in 1910. Following years of struggle, their people finally obtained land near Havre, Montana, becoming the only Chippewa-Cree reservation in the state. Today's Rocky Boy Reservation has over three thousand Ojibwe, Cree, and Métis tribal members. A long history of alliance and intermarriage has reduced the distinctions among the groups. The languages in use on the reservation include Cree, Mitchif (a mixture of Cree, Ojibwe, and French), and English. Stone Child Community College, one of several tribal colleges in the state, was established in 1982. Other enterprises include a development company and facilities centering around camping, fishing, and skiing.

The Little Shell Band of Chippewa represent another migration of Ojibwes into present-day Montana. When United States government officials conducted a census of the Turtle Mountain Chippewa as part of treaty negotiations with the groups in the late 1800s, many of the leader Little Shell's people were away hunting buffalo. The federal government refused to count many members of the band, along with Mitchif, as part of Turtle Mountain. Turtle Mountain's population was thus undercounted, disenfranchising about five thousand tribal members who were absent during the census. The government then reduced the reservation's land base to two townships in 1884.

Little Shell continued to seek a homeland for his followers, traveling between North Dakota and Montana until his death in 1900. Today, descendants of the Little Shell Band of Chippewa live in a number of non-Indian communities in Montana. They are governed by a Tribal Council, with an office in Havre and an office for economic development in Helena.

The Landless Chippewa migrated to present-day Montana, settling in communities such as those in the Lewistown area of the state. Today, their descendants live in areas of north-central Montana without reservation or trust lands. Along with some of Little Shell's descendants, the Landless Chippewa are seeking federal recognition for their people.

Turtle Mountain Allotment Community. Another group of Ojibwes in Montana became known as the Turtle Mountain Allotment Community. Following negotiations between the federal government and Turtle Mountain in 1892, tribal members from that band took allotments on public domain lands in North Dakota and Montana. Montana's allotments, in this case, numbered nearly two thousand at 160 acres (64 hectares) each. After losing their allotment lands, some of the tribal people returned to North Dakota. Others, however, remained in Montana. Today, the Montana Allotment Community includes approximately one thousand Turtle Mountain Ojibwe.

Canadian Ojibwe

Ojibwes in Canada include both woodland and Plains groups on reserves in Ontario, Manitoba, and Saskatchewan. They also reside off-reserve, in urban areas such as Toronto and Winnipeg and in other communities, including some that have not received federal recognition. The treaty-making period and federal policies diminished landholdings of the tribal group just as they did in the United States. Approximately seventy bands of Ojibwe have government status in Canada. In southern Ontario alone are around three dozen Ojibwe reserves, including Walpole Island, Sarnia, Saugeen, Cape Croker, Rama, Parry Island, Garden River, Sheshegwaning, Sheguianda, Wikwemikong, and New Credit.

The westernmost Ojibwe reserves in Canada are located in Saskatchewan, where as many as a dozen can be found near North Battleford. Other reserves in the province, along with those in Alberta, include combined populations of Ojibwes and Crees. Manitoba includes Ojibwe reserves between the Winnipeg and Poplar Rivers as well as others on inland lakes and still others with combined Ojibwe-Cree populations.

— P. F. Molin / L. Roy / C. K. Washburne

SEE ALSO:

Alberta; Canada, Native–Non-Native Relations in; Fishing Rights; Gaming; General Allotment Act; Indian Claims Commission Act; Indian New Deal (Indian Reorganization Act); Manitoba; Métis; Michigan; Minnesota; Missions for Indians, Christian; Montana; Nonrecognized Communities; North Dakota; Ojibwe Literature, Contemporary; Ontario; Ottawa; Potawatomi; Riel, Louis; Saskatchewan; Wisconsin.

SUGGESTED READINGS:

Eagle/Walking Turtle. *Indian America: A Traveler's Companion*. Santa Fe, NM: John Muir Publications, 1993.

Formen, Werner, and Norman Bancroft-Hunt. *The Indians of the Great Plains*. London: Orbis Publishing Limited, 1981.